PSYCHOANALYTIC INQUIRY

A Topical Journal for Mental Health Professionals

Volume 25 | 2005 | Number 2

Reconsidering the Work of Joseph Sandler: The Affect of Safety, the Representational World, and Role Responsiveness

Prologue

In the early 1960s, Joseph Sandler, trained in ego psychology and working at the Hampstead Clinic with Anna Freud, began writing papers that reduced the chasm between psychoanalytic theory, clinical experience, and psychoanalytic research. He began exploring the characteristics of the superego and ego ideal. The ego psychology of the time was inadequate to explain his clinical observations. He understood that many of the concepts of object relations theory and Kleinian psychology explained his clinical observations and were congruous with ego psychology.

During the next four decades, with courage and creativity, Sandler wrote papers that contributed to the depolarization and pluralism of many psychoanalytic models and concepts. He created bridges that spanned psychoanalysis with cognitive and developmental sciences. He developed research models that helped him expand his ideas. The three concepts that most characterize Sandler's creativity are the affect of safety, the representational world, and role responsiveness.

The Editors of *Psychoanalytic Inquiry* devote this entire issue to Joseph Sandler's work because it celebrates the best of psychoanalysis. It exemplifies his devotion to improving the understanding of the complexity of the clinical experience. Because of Sandler's background in human development and child analysis, he understood that the analysis rests on an evolutionary process which is set in the here and now. He appreciated that in the clinical situation affects must play a central role guided by the development of ideals and values. He realized that the psychoanalytic theory that he was originally given had gaping deficiencies, but enormous value and meaning which he could use as the foundation for creativity and innovation.

We asked six contributors to write about Sandler's three major contributions: the affect of safety, the representational world, and role responsiveness. And two discussants of their papers explore the creativity and scope of Sandler's contribution to psychoanalysis.

Peter Fonagy leads off with a comprehensive review of Sandler's work. He describes the "quiet revolution" within psychoanalysis that Sandler prompted in the latter half of the 20th century. This revolution created areas of commonality between ego psychology, object relations theory, Kleinian psychology, and the interpersonal psychology which we continue to evolve.

Alex Holder writes about the development of Sandler's views of feeling states and intrapsychic mechanisms and processes especially related to internal objects and internal object relations. Holder explores Sandler's use of a variety of concepts and views.

Otto Kernberg contends that object relations theory provides a model for the integration of metapsychology, the psychoanalytic process, and the clinical situation more completely than a model of drive and conflict alone. He believes that Joseph Sandler has been more instrumental than any other analyst in influencing this integration. To Sandler, the centrality of affect, the representational world, and internalized object relations are seen as the underpinnings of the ego, superego, and id while the centrality of affect bridges experience with the abstractions of metapsychology.

Glen Gabbard delves into the development of Sandler's ideas on countertransference. He discusses Sandler's familiarity with the classical, object relations, and Kleinian perspectives that enabled him to create bridges that led to the development of role responsiveness. Gabbard also elaborates on his view that a common ground has evolved within psychoanalysis on the significance of the analyst's reactions in the analytic dyad.

Arnold Cooper explores Sandler's formulation of the representational world that has served as a background for the integration and development of many theoretical and clinical views within psychoanalysis. The representational world has helped analysts focus on the creation of one's inner world and the meanings that are generated from it in contrast to an inner world that is simply a linear reflection of the external world. The dynamics of the representational world enable the current understanding of brain physiology. Finally, Cooper demonstrates the enormous value of the representational world in clinical work.

I tackle Sandler's three-box model, which embraces the representational world and the affect of safety, exploring some of the current concepts of a developing self.

The issue concludes with discussions of the papers by Henry Smith and Joseph Lichtenberg.

Melvin Bornstein, M.D.
Issue Editor

An Overview of Joseph Sandler's Key Contributions to Theoretical and Clinical Psychoanalysis

PETER FONAGY, PH.D., F.B.A.

Joseph Sandler was instrumental in bringing about what Ogden (1992) has termed the "quiet revolution" in psychoanalytic theory over the past several decades. His accomplishments reflected his capacity to combine empirical research skills with the highest order of understanding of psychoanalytic theory. From the more traditional frame of reference acquired through his analytic training, Sandler gradually evolved a complex integration of ego psychology and object relations theory that has become increasingly dominant. Throughout this process, Sandler strove to keep theory tied to clinical activity. While most analysts pay lip service to the intimate relationship of theory and practice, Sandler, using the Hampstead Psychoanalytic Index as his framework, researched the applicability of psychoanalytic concepts to the clinical setting. This resulted in reconceptualizations of some of the basic building blocks of psychoanalysis. His training as an experimental psychologist gave him a fresh perspective on traditional concepts, which he supported and altered on the basis of empirical research. His immersion in child development at the Anna Freud Centre also influenced his intellectual development.

Peter Fonagy, Ph.D., F.B.A. is Freud Memorial Professor of Psychoanalysis, University College London; Chief Executive, The Anna Freud Centre, London.

To ADEQUATELY REVIEW SANDLER'S PSYCHOANALYTIC CONTRIBUTIONS requires an ability to mold and synthesize psychoanalytic concepts that probably only Sandler himself possessed. Highlighted here are some of Sandler's most important contributions to encourage readers to explore further for themselves.

Representation and Affects

The Representational World

The most important new psychoanalytic concept introduced by Sandler is his frame of reference for the representational world. Described fully in a paper coauthored with Bernard Rosenblatt (Sandler and Rosenblatt, 1962), the representational world had earlier formed the background to his 1960 paper on the superego (Sandler, 1960c), as well as others (e.g., Sandler, 1962). Sandler's concept of the representational world is rooted, among others, in the work of Piaget (1936, 1937), Jacobson's (1953a, b, 1954a, b, c) concept of self-representation and Head's (1926) notion of body schema. The representational world is one of a family of psychological models that came into its own with the cognitive revolution in psychology, spurred by the analogy between the human mind and digital computers, long after Sandler's adoption of the concept. The use of the mental representational idea in cognitive science has led psychodynamically oriented psychologists, as well as psychoanalysts, to adopt Sandler's notion as the dominant framework for the conceptualization of the internal representation of object relationships (e.g., Bowlby, 1973, 1980; Kernberg, 1976; Stolorow and Atwood, 1979; Stern, 1985; Blatt and Behrends, 1987; Horowitz, 1991; Westen, 1991).

Sandler's internal working model antedates but resembles Bowlby's formulation. Both owe an intellectual debt to the cognitive revolution in psychology in the early 1960s (Gardner, 1985). Both view relationship representations as consisting "in essence, of a set of expectations relating to the mother's appearance and activities" (Sandler, 1960c, p. 147). In Sandler's (1962) account, representations of self and other have a "shape"; they also have a critical affective component that helps to organize and integrate sensations and perceptions arising from interpersonal experience. Once a self-representation is formed, object representations can be established. Sandler's metaphor links the representational model to structural theory: the ego is the theater, and representations are characters on the stage. We are aware of the characters enacting the drama but remain blissfully ignorant of the essential props required to stage the play.

This idea enabled Sandler to differentiate some basic psychoanalytic concepts. For example, in introjection there is a change in status of parent representations that does not involve a change in self-representation. In incorporation, on the other hand, the self-representation changes to resemble the perceived image of the object. Identification is a momentary fusion of self- and object representations that preserves their boundaries and separateness. An instinctual wish may be seen as a temporary modification in the representation of the self or the object; conflict can result in the exclusion of these representations from consciousness. Defenses rearrange the contents of the representational world (e.g., projection modifies the shape of the object representation to make it resemble the unconscious self-representation). Similarly, primary narcissism is the libidinal cathexis of the self-representation; object love is the transfer of this cathexis to the object representation. Secondary narcissism is the withdrawal of libidinal cathexis from the object representation to the self-representation.

In his early papers, Sandler saw no inconsistency between the notion of the representational world and classical Freudian metapsychology. But his meticulous, systematic development of the representational world framework would be the bedrock of the "quiet revolution" in psychoanalytic thought. He was not the first to bring psychoanalysis implicitly into line with discoveries of other mind sciences (e.g., Jacobson, 1964), but he was the first to do so by offering a comprehensive alternative conceptualization of psychoanalysis without simultaneously claiming to have reinvented the entire discipline. This balance of radical innovation clothed as minimalist innovation was the hallmark of Sandler's brilliant contribution.

The Concept of Feeling States

Sandler revised psychoanalytic theory by placing feeling states rather than psychic energy at the center of the psychoanalytic theory of motivation. In a chapter on the role of affect in psychoanalytic theory, Sandler (1972a) stated unequivocally that "while drives, needs, emotional forces, and other influences arising from within the body are highly important in determining behavior, from the point of view of psychological functioning they exert their effect through changes in feeling" (p. 296). Sandler saw the entire ideational content of the experiential field as embedded within a matrix of feeling states that gives direction to all adaptation.

This emphasis on feeling states created a bridge between classical drive theories and object relations theories. Sandler's assumption that feeling states are subjective experiences representing a state of self in relation to another person was key. Many creative contributors to the study of object relationships, particularly early mother–infant interactions, have gone on to make extensive use of Sandler's model (e.g., Stern, 1985; Emde, 1988) as an alternative to poorly fitting drive theory accounts.

In 1978, Sandler lectured on unconscious wishes and human relationships, making explicit his conviction that the wish is the basic unit of psychoanalytic discourse, whereas instincts and drives are basic psychological tendencies. In further papers (e.g., Sandler and Sandler, 1978), the break with classical drive theory became explicit. Sandler traced the historical progression of his ideas in a paper delivered in 1985 in New York (Sandler, 1989). For Sandler, affects drove wishes, which in turn drove actions, and could be seen at the root of conflict. A major departure from the most mechanistic aspects of the ego psychology tradition was now under way, a process that culminated in this tradition's eventual rejection (Schafer, 1976, 1978). While Sandler was perhaps one of the first to focus motivation-theory building on feeling states rather than drives, he was by no means the only one. Among those who also contributed to this shift were several major figures in the world of infant psychopathology (Spitz, 1965; Emde, 1980a, b), cognitive science (Rosenblatt and Thickstun, 1970, 1977; Peterfreund, 1971), as well as pioneers in psychoanalytic work with the severe end of adult personality disturbance (Kernberg, 1975, 1976; Masterson, 1985). Sandler was unique in his capacity to maintain a seamless contact with the work of Freud and a commitment to retaining the key components of the "old" metapsychology where it was still useful and productive.

The Superego, the Ego Ideal, and the Ideal Self

In a critical and well-known paper, Sandler (1960c) radically revised the concept of the superego. He introduced the "preautonomous superego schema," altering classical Freudian formulations of the superego and Kleinian notions (e.g., Klein, 1927, 1933, 1958), to explain how preoedipal children can develop moral object-related behavior. More important, he showed that the superego contains approving and permissive, as well as prohibiting, features by giving the child a background feeling of being loved. Structuralization of the superego remains associated with the Oedipus complex and implies the capacity to invoke these affective states without the supervision of the parental object.

As part of the processing of case material in the Hampstead Index, Sandler, along with Alex Holder and Dale Meers (Sandler, Holder, and Meers, 1963), uncovered major ambiguities in the concept of the ego ideal (e.g., a conscience, an ideal self-representation, and ideal parental introjects). Applying the model of the representational world, they suggested that the ego ideal was a version of the self that had the desired shape of the self. This representation arose as a compromise between desired instinctual gratification and the child's need to gain the love and approval of parents or introjects. The discrepancy between the self and the ideal self-representation was seen as inversely proportional to self-esteem. Shame, for example, could arise from a failure "to live up to ideal standards" (Sandler et al., 1963, p. 157), whereas guilt arose out of a perceived difference between the ideal self and the self as dictated by introjects.

Pain and Depression

In two papers, Sandler and Joffe (Joffe and Sandler, 1965; Sandler and Joffe, 1965a, b) reconsidered depression from a representational-world perspective. They argued that the term previously had been used imprecisely, without distinguishing between states of unhappiness, misery (pain), and depression as affective responses. They argued that psychic pain may be understood as the discrepancy between an actual state of self and an ideal based on memories or fantasies. This discrepancy was seen as common to all forms of unpleasure, including anxiety. Aggression was a normal response to such an inconsistency.

The individual gradually develops an appreciation of reality that entails relinquishing previously enjoyed states of satisfaction and departing from magical and omnipotent experiences—optimally with minimal pain. Giving up ideal states may be more analogous to the process of mourning rather than depression. However, ideal states of well-being involve mental object representations. Loss of the object may be usefully translated then to mean loss of a state of self for which the object was a vehicle. Depressive responses may follow when the individual does not respond to psychic pain with an adequate discharge of aggression. The adaptive response is individuation, a process of working through that involves abandoning the pursuit of lost ideal states and adopting new ones that are syntonic with reality, as well as with internal states. This process occurs throughout life but is developmentally typical of particular stages determined by biology and culture.

The depressive response—capitulation in the face of pain—is the opposite of individuation. It is maladaptive in that it may dull psychic pain because of the associated inhibition, but "it is not aimed at recovery" (Joffe and Sandler, 1965, p. 423). Depression is thus a final common pathway to a wide range of influences that can include constitutional factors as well as environmental and intrapsychic ones.

The Background of Safety

In a 1959 presentation, Sandler (1960a) introduced the background of safety, a revolutionary concept that placed the ego in a positive framework of trying to maximize safety or security rather than to avoid anxiety. Although Sandler recognized the inverse complementarity of anxiety and safety, he showed that the pursuit of safety is an overarching construct, compatible with instinct theory, that has the capacity to organize defenses, perceptions, and fantasies. In addition, Sandler reaffirmed the status of instinctual drives as "prime motivators of behavior" (p. 365). Nevertheless, this concept provided a motivational framework that was far better articulated with the interpersonal object relations tradition than a simple drive-theory model.

Patterns of perception can represent safety, so success can be perceived as a threat, and failure can become linked to feelings of familiarity and safety. Thus the feeling of safety can override displeasure in terms of pain and suffering. The apparently simple concept of safety has proved essential not only to Sandler's elaboration of object relations theory but also to other areas. For example, in a later paper, Joffe and Sandler (1968) applied it to autonomy, which was seen as a reflection of the range of strategies available to maintain one's basic feeling of safety in the face of threats of disruption from the drives, the superego, or the external world.

Sandler's concept of safety resembles Hermann's (1923) clinging instinct and Bowlby's (1973) secure-base notion, but for the latter authors, safety was a biological force,[1] whereas for Sandler it was distinct and lacked the excitement normally associated with drive gratification. In fact, Sandler (1989) opposed the two, demonstrating that the urge to gain feelings of well-being and safety must be stronger than instinctual gratification to keep the latter in check when its expression implies danger. Safety is the most radical example of Sandler's rethinking of motivation in terms of feeling states in place of drives.

A Theory of Trauma

Prompted in part by the difficulty of defining trauma in absolute terms either as an intrapsychic experience of being overwhelmed or as a particular category of external events, Sandler (1967) revised the concept. In an important theoretical advance, he specified that the pathological sequelae of trauma do not depend on the child's initial experience of helplessness in the face of the event but rather on the child's posttraumatic condition. He suggested that the clinical sequelae of trauma may be due to the continuing strain on the ego, determined principally by the degree of inner conflict that remains after the trauma, crippling personality growth and leading to the development of borderline, delinquent, or psychotic pathology.

---

[1] Sandler (1995) integrated his accounts with those of attachment theory and research.

The Basic Psychoanalytic Model

Sandler and Joffe's work culminated in a paper (Sandler and Joffe, 1969) on the basic psychoanalytic model in which they introduced a number of critical distinctions to psychoanalytic psychology. Perhaps the most important was distinction of the experiential from the nonexperiential realms of psychoanalytic theorization. Whereas the former referred to Sandler and Joffe's representational model, the latter entailed mechanisms, structures, and apparatuses. The nonexperiential is inherently nonconscious, although it is not repressed or dynamically inhibited. The distinction between a fantasy (conscious or unconscious) and the organized function underpinning it (fantasying) remains an evocative example.

The model makes clear that experience is not the agent of change; change is brought about by structures in the nonexperiential realm, which cause corresponding changes in the experiential. Thus self-representation cannot be an agent, but it is an entity that determines how mechanisms of the mind behave. This paper located Sandler's model in a relatively clear position vis-à-vis Greenberg and Mitchell's (1983) dichotomy between drive and relational models. Sandler's model placed relational formulations within the framework of a structural psychology, albeit considerably modified from that of Freud, Hartmann, Kris, Loewenstein, and Rapaport. While modifying structural theory, Sandler refused to abandon the ambition of psychoanalysis as a general psychology of structures and basic mental processes.

In later papers, Sandler extensively used this important distinction. For example, in a paper on "The Structure of Internal Objects and Internal Object Relations," Sandler (1990) made clear his view of internal objects as "structures" within the nonexperiential realm, albeit constructed out of subjective experience, conscious or unconscious. Once created, such nonexperiential structures can modify subjective experience, including the child's experience of the actual objects. The distinction between the experiential and nonexperiential realms remained a key concern for Sandler. In his very last paper, presented on the occasion of Hanna Segal's 80th birthday, he discussed Dr. Segal's attempt to link Chomsky's model of language to the notion of unconscious fantasy. Sandler was quick to point out that the deep structure of the unconscious was inherently nonexperiential.

From a somewhat different perspective, I have advanced with colleagues a notion that psychic change can be understood as occurring at two levels. Relatively rapid changes were changes of mental representation, changes in the shape of the self-representation, the representation of the other, or the links between the two. This corresponds to Sandler's experiential realm. Psychic change also occurs at the mental-process level. Mental processes are the psychological mechanisms that generate mental representation. We have used the metaphor of a musical instrument: the tune is the mental representation, the instrument is the mental process. Changes in mental process are nonexperiential by definition. Alterations in the general shape, quality, coherence, and integrity of particular categories of mental representation are noticed—for example, those associated with affect, with perceptions of the object, with the contents of the mind in self and other. These nonexperiential changes are hard-won, but perhaps more lasting, and they link to the traditional construct of structural change.

Representations of Object Relations, Past and Present

Actualization and Role Responsiveness

A key concept in the second phase of Sandler's writing was actualization in the sense of "to make actual" or "to realize an action." Sandler (1976b) traced the roots of actualization to chapter 7 of Freud's (1900) *Interpretation of Dreams,* which discussed wish fulfillment in fantasy as a repetition of the perception linked with need satisfaction. Sandler suggested that dreaming provides satisfaction because the dreamer observes his own dream, thus achieving an identity of perception.

The idea of actualization was put to excellent use in a paper on role responsiveness that appeared about the same time (Sandler, 1976a). In this highly influential work, Sandler showed how patients wishing to actualize an unconscious fantasy create role relationships. They cast themselves and the analyst in a specific relationship that actualizes a variety of unconscious needs and defenses. The patients attempt to act on the external world and bring about changes to make it conform to an unconscious fantasy. Sandler (1976a) suggested that analysts should allow themselves a "free-floating responsiveness," whereby they accept—at least in part—and reflect on the role assigned to them and put it to good use in understanding their patients. Of critical importance here is that a part of the patient's mind is devoted to scanning and understanding the total analyst–patient situation because it is the entire role relationship that represents an identity of perception with the unconscious fantasy. Countertransference then must be understood as part of this process, which extends beyond the boundaries of the clinical situation and reflects the regular functioning of the unconscious mind.

Internal Object Relations

In a seminal paper with Anne-Marie Sandler (1978), Joseph Sandler demonstrated the immense heuristic value of his expanded notion of motivation. The frame of reference provided by representation and the concept of identity of perception offered a new and ingenious theory of internal object representations. He showed how wishful fantasies are represented as interactions between self and object, the basic aim being to bring about a primary affective "good" state while distancing a bad one. Thus the object plays as important a role as the self in the mental representation that embodies the wish. Object relationships are thus fulfillment, not only of instinctual wishes, but also of the needs for safety, reassurance, and affirmation. Such needs accompany the actualization of a wished-for childhood relationship, albeit heavily disguised at times.

Overt relationships are derivatives of underlying wishful-fantasy role relationships. As these representations are reinforced during the course of development, personality is formed and the individual becomes increasingly inflexible in the roles demanded of self and others. Character traits can thus be understood as well-established role-responsive structures that actualize a wished-for representation of a relationship, which in turn is a derivative of one existing in unconscious fantasy (Sandler, 1981).

The psychological structures that represent these wished-for relationships are not simply perceptions of the interaction between child and parent. The perceptions of these relationships are subject to defensive transformations resulting from the ego's need to gratify yet defend against unconscious wishes. The defensive modification occurs in response to the underlying intrapsychic mental representation. Because the structures that embody both the self and the internal representation are determined in part by the child's fantasy life, the object, as represented in the child's mind, is a distortion derived sometimes almost entirely from fantasy constructions. The image of the object may be distorted so that it represents split-off aspects of the unconscious self-image that would normally arouse unpleasant affect (e.g., feelings of guilt or shame). Thus the manifest relationship that emerges in the psychoanalytic setting (or in everyday encounters) is most frequently a heavily disguised version of the unconscious fantasy—originally represented in relationship terms—rather than a simple repetition of internalized patterns of interpersonal relations. Nevertheless, the resulting internalized pattern may serve to create the unconscious illusion that the love object is present.

The remarkable usefulness of this framework is well illustrated by its power to provide a satisfactory account of some of the most puzzling aspects of human behavior. Many "dialogues," as Sandler (1990) termed them, between self and object are extremely painful yet paradoxically retained by patients. He pointed out that they provide safety because they allow the patient to continue experiencing the presence of the object. They are necessary, even if persecuting or guilt-provoking, because in fantasy the internal object can continue through this presence to function as the embodiment of unacceptable aspects of self-representation, thus enhancing the individual's experience of overall safety in terms of the mental economy of affect. In addition, their continuity may enhance safety through the mere familiarity of their presence.

Projective Identification

Sandler's (1987) formulation of projective identification was a particularly useful attempt to link a dominant Kleinian notion to the sophisticated representational point of view now generally adopted by most theorists. Sandler saw clinical observations in which the psychoanalyst appears to be experiencing a feeling more appropriately attributable to the patient as a wishful fantasy of the patient that included the analyst. The fantasy involved modification of the representation of the object in the patient's mind so that it contains unwanted aspects of the self-representation. To actualize the fantasy, the patient attempts to make the behavior of the analyst conform with the distorted representation. Retaining self-object boundaries is essential in order for the mechanism to fulfill its defensive function of dissociating unwanted aspects of the self while maintaining the illusion of controlling them through control of the object.

This concept may also be illustrated within the context of the transgenerational transmission of representations evident in infancy (Fraiberg, Adelson, and Shapiro, 1975; Sandler, 1994). The mother's interaction with her child is based on her representations of past attachment relationships. In such encounters, the mother may modify the representation of her child, making it identical to an unwanted aspect of herself. She may then manipulate the infant to behave consistently with her distorted representation. Naturally, this process works both ways; infants may, from time to time, be obliged to distort their representation of their caregivers in order to deal with unmanageable affect and bring about behavioral reactions in the adults that confirm the accuracy of their mental representation. The model is basically a dynamic one, in that what the child experiences as unmanageable is by no means absolute, but, rather, strongly dependent on what is perceived to be experienced by the caregiver as unmanageable and unacceptable in the child. Gradually, through this process, the child's self-representation may increasingly resemble that of the caregiver. The dialectic process that occurs intrapsychically between self- and other representations (within the framework of the representation of the interactions between them) advances an isomorphic set of representations in the two individuals.

We have found Sandler's model of projective identification enormously valuable in understanding disorganized attachment. Sandler does not distinguish between projective identifications where an internal representation of a relationship is enacted from a more primitive situation where an unwanted part of the self is experienced without rather than within. Elsewhere we have suggested that a dialectic model of self-development, where the self is seen as shaped by the mirroring other (Davidson, 1980; Cavell, 1994) inevitably generates a disorganized, fragmented self-structure when the other is less than perfect in mirroring the self. As this is almost invariably the case, it is inconceivable that the self-structure should be flawless. It is generally accepted that when mirroring is imperfect it is the other that is internalized (introjected) into the self, yet comes to be experienced as part of the self (Winnicott, 1956; Jacobson, 1964). The externalization of this alien part of the self through projective identification is reassuring because the split-off part of the self can be experienced as being outside in the object controlled and nudged into behaving in line with the intended projection (Fonagy et al., 2002). In this context, what may be more crucial than the relationship that is created through projective identification is the sense of safety which the experience of seeing the disturbing part of oneself outside rather than inside can provide. We have suggested that the more disorganized the early attachment relationship, the more fragmented the self-structure, the more projective identification will serve a simple evacuating function rather than the creation of a role relationship where a self–other relationship is externalized.

The Three-Box Model

In a series of scholarly papers published in the 1970s, Sandler and his coworkers (chiefly Alex Holder and Chris Dare) made the most coherent attempt in the history of the discipline to crystallize the frames of reference of classical psychoanalysis (Sandler, Holder, and Dare, 1972, 1973a, b, c, 1975, 1976; Sandler, Dare, and Holder, 1972b, 1974, 1978, 1982; Sandler, 1974). This work culminated in an important paper by Sandler and Sandler (1984) which highlighted the inconsistencies that have arisen as a direct consequence of the concurrent use of these incompatible frameworks.

Sandler and Sandler (1984) proposed a far more coherent frame of reference to distinguish two aspects of unconscious functioning. The first system or "box" consists of "those infantile reactions, infantile wishes, or wishful fantasies that develop early in life and are the outcome of all the transformations that defensive activities and modifying processes have brought about during that period" (p. 418). This system is the child within the adult, primitive in terms of mental structure but by no means restricted to sexual and aggressive impulses. Sandler and Sandler (1987) see the system as composed of unconscious fantasies with wish-fulfilling, problem-solving, reassuring, and defensive aspects. Indeed, it embodies the ego of the young child as well as the superego formation of the early years. From the point of view of cognitive sophistication, representations within this structure are less well elaborated and are dominated by childhood theories. Never directly accessible to consciousness, the system is essentially unchangeable. What is changeable, though, is how the adult psyche accommodates derivatives of the past unconscious.

The second system or "box" is also unconscious; representations within it may be more or less subject to censorship. It is equivalent to Freud's unconscious ego, but also contains unconscious representations normally assigned to the superego. It differs from the first system in that it is oriented to the present rather than the past. Conflict-solving compromises are created within it, facilitating intrapsychic adaptation; the most important of these is the creation and modification of current unconscious fantasies and thoughts. Whereas external stimuli applied to the first system may trigger past unconscious fantasy, the second system involves the constant modification of representations of self- and object interactions that are less peremptory and disruptive than the mental products of the first system. It is cognitively more involved and more closely linked with representations of the present-day reality. It also shares the property of unconscious systems in tolerating contradictions.

The nature of the second censorship, at the border of the second and third systems, differs qualitatively from that on the border of the first and second. Whereas the latter may be conceived of as analogous to Freud's repression barrier, the former is principally oriented toward avoiding shame, embarrassment, and humiliation. The third system is conscious and only irrational to the degree that may be licensed by social convention.

The clinical significance of this distinction is self-evident. The first box is a continuation of the past in the present. It lacks cognizance of the need for adaptation because it is based on infantile aspects of the child's self. The second box is the present unconscious, consisting of here-and-now adaptations to the conflicts and anxieties triggered in the first box. It follows from this model that material in this part of the mind is more likely to be accessible to interpretation so it must be considered appropriate for intervention—all the more so because the analyst's authority positions him or her to overcome the second censorship by providing an atmosphere of tolerance that weakens the inhibition based on shame, embarrassment, and humiliation. Interpretations, even in a transferential context, that attempt to immediately access putative, peremptory fantasies or to directly address the child within, without first addressing their derivatives in the second system, inevitably muddle the two forms of the unconscious and reduce the impact of the intervention.

Unconscious Fantasy

Sandler first distinguished between fantasies that are descriptively unconscious and fantasies that arise as a consequence of the act of repression and so may be called dynamically unconscious in an early paper on the metapsychology of fantasy (Sandler and Nagera, 1963). Fantasies originating in the system unconscious provide the ideational content of unsatisfied wishes but do not constitute wish fulfillment; rather, they represent the gratifying experience. In contrast, preconscious fantasies are attempts at wish fulfillment or are derivatives of wish fulfillment fantasies. Preconscious fantasies may, of course, reflect the failure of wish fulfillment in that they incorporate defensively modified derivatives. What is dynamically unconscious acts as the source of what is preconscious or descriptively unconscious, the latter striving toward consciousness in order to achieve identity of perception.

Sandler and Nagera's paper also distinguished between conscious fantasy (or daydreams through which the loosening of reality testing created a wish-fulfilling situation in the imagination known to be not real); preconscious, descriptively unconscious, fantasy (nonconscious daydreams); and unconscious fantasy (repressed preconscious fantasies that, once repressed, function like memories of gratification, deserving the term "fantasy" only in that they were the source of conscious or preconscious fantasies). The process of unconscious fantasizing was seen as an ego function located in the nonconscious ego and involving both childlike and more mature forms of thought—that is, a constant "back-and-forth" movement within the system preconscious. Sandler, in a chapter on sexual fantasies in 1975 and in the important paper in 1983 on the links between psychoanalytic theory and practice, reinforced the importance of recognizing that not all unconscious wish fulfillment fantasies could be traced back to sexual or aggressive instincts; rather, some may be fulfilling wishes for safety, protecting against threats to self-esteem presented by feelings of guilt and shame or even from the external world.

With the development of the three-box model, the notion of unconscious fantasy could be elaborated further (Sandler and Sandler, 1986). Unconscious fantasies in the second box (the present unconscious) function adaptationally by involving constant modifications of self- and object representations, thus restoring the individual's equilibrium again and again, much like a gyroscope stabilizes a physical object through centrifugal and centripetal forces. The peremptory urges and fantasies of the past unconscious disturb mental equilibrium but are worked on (elaborated) in the second system to restore homeostasis. Wishes and impulses that arise in the deeper layers of the present unconscious threaten the individual's current equilibrium. These fantasies are dynamically kept from consciousness by the internalized social judgment of the second censorship. In reaction to narcissistic hurt, for example, grandiose omnipotent fantasies help restore equilibrium but become inconsistent with the child's more mature thoughts so are kept out of consciousness; if allowed in, they are extensively modified (made plausible through rationalization). Unconscious fantasies modified by defensive activity are gratified by making reality consistent with them via externalization (actualization) and by making such actions plausible through rationalization. Psychotic phenomena have a similar reequilibrating function but sacrifice social plausibility.

Clinical Concepts

Transference

In an insightful monograph with Chris Dare and Alex Holder based on a series of papers in the *British Journal of Psychiatry* in the 1970s, Sandler carefully scrutinized many fundamental clinical psychoanalytic concepts (Sandler, Dare, and Holder, 1973). A productive collaboration with Ursula Dreher resulted in a new edition of this widely used text. Many of its concepts deserve presentation here, but because of limitations of space I shall concentrate on only a couple of the topics.

In a 1969 paper with a number of colleagues at the Anna Freud Centre, Sandler revised the concept of transference (Sandler et al., 1969). The paper contrasted transferences in the analytic situation with transferences in everyday life, illustrating the problems that may arise from applying a metapsychological frame of reference to a clinical concept. The clinical and technical use of the term covers a broad spectrum of experiences, all of which concern object relationships in general. Sandler and his colleagues identified a number of phenomena representing dimensions of transference that should be distinguished for both technical and conceptual reasons (e.g., displacement of wishes, conflicts, or reactions to others, externalization of parts of the representational system, character transferences, the so-called real relationship, and the therapeutic alliance). They reformulated the question of what is and is not transference by asking, "What dimensions of relationship enter into the special and artificial analytic situation, and how are these involved in the process of treatment?" (p. 643). Thus the repetition of past relationships with defenses against them is only one dimension of a complex phenomenon.

The elaboration of the model of internal object relations led Sandler (1990) to reformulate the concept of transference. He saw patients as gratifying, through actualization in the analytic situation, their unconscious wishful fantasies via a disguised identity of perception (Sandler, 1976b, 1990). The recognition of these internal object relationships in the transference does not constitute a perception by the analyst, but rather a construction, a framework imposed on the material brought by the patient.

Sandler further elaborated on the significance of this distinction. Constructions concerning the inner world of the patient pertain to a current state of affairs, not to memories, even if that state of affairs is marked by childlike features and clearly involves an object of childhood concern (an omnipotent parental figure or a dangerous and persecutory one). Reconstruction, although frequently confused with construction, provides a temporal perspective by rediscovering the state of affairs of the historical past.

The distinction between the present and past unconscious also aided the understanding of transference (Sandler and Sandler, 1984). Unconscious transference fantasies are part of the present unconscious with its aim of restoring psychic equilibrium by manipulating self- and object representations. They are kept from consciousness and expressed in displaced forms because they violate the principles of the second censorship, protecting consciousness from shame and humiliation. Sandler and Sandler (1987) point out that the patient's constant striving to actualize wishful fantasies in the present unconscious makes the analysis of transference the most convincing route to elucidation of the present unconscious. The hierarchical layering of unconscious fantasies in the second "box" implies that interpretation of the transference should be as close as possible to the current central conflict and to the patient's immediate resistance. The present should always be interpreted before the past. The past should only be foregrounded to illuminate what is occurring currently.

Within this framework, the analyst and patient are seen as jointly creating an extended model of the patient's self and world. As a result, the patient acquires a perspective on the childlike part of the self, which is frequently repudiated but made acceptable in the clinical context by the analyst's tolerant attitude.

Countertransference and the Vicissitudes of Guilt

In a paper integrating their writing on internal object relations and the past and present unconscious, Sandler and Sandler (1987) presented a brief but highly sophisticated portrait of the role of guilt in psychoanalytic work. They distinguished guilt accessible to interpretation, seen as part of the present unconscious, from hypothetical primitive guilt embedded in the archaic fantasies of the past unconscious which cannot be perceived, only conceived and reconstructed.

The Sandlers note numerous maneuvers to protect against the destabilizing influence of guilt. These all aim to modify the representation of the selfobject interaction (the unconscious fantasy) in order to restore homeostasis. They may include actual feelings of guilt that are experienced about something else rather than the original source. In masochistic reactions, guilt is atoned for by directing aggression and sadism against the self. Role responsiveness may play a part by provoking the criticism of others when the unconscious fantasy of the self as being reproached or held in contempt by the introject "leaks out" without the patient's awareness. The analyst may have countertransference awareness of critical feelings toward the patient. Sometimes the modified fantasy may mitigate guilt by further modifying the fantasy so that it depicts unjust criticism; the patient may actualize this fantasy by provoking unjust accusations, leading to feelings of entitlement and self-vindication. All these enactments may be understood by the analyst but not perceived by the patient without interpretation.

Regression

Sandler's contributions are all strongly developmentally oriented. Nowhere is this clearer than in the papers on regression. The first (Sandler and Joffe, 1965b) dealt with obsessional phenomena in children and evoked the concept of the function of regression of aspects of the ego (p. 145). This model suggested that particular modes of ego functioning may be associated with varying degrees of pleasure, thus creating the potential to return to that mode of functioning in a way analogous to drive regression. Obsessional children manifest a "particular style of the perceptual and cognitive functions of the ego" that indicates the ego's fixation in the second and third year of life (p. 436). In Sandler's papers on depression and individuation (Joffe and Sandler, 1965; Sandler and Joffe, 1965a, b), regression is described as a response to frustration and suffering that arises from the need to give up early magical and omnipotent ideal states in favor of an appreciation of reality; it attempts to stave off helplessness and its possible sequel, the depressive response. Modes of ego functioning may produce feelings of safety and mastery and can thus exert as much backward pull as do libidinal fixations.

Sandler and Joffe (1967) were the first to recognize fully the major theoretical implications of Freud's (1933) notion of persistence when he emphasized that psychological

> structures are in the normal course of events never lost, but rather that new and auxiliary structures of increasing complexity are created, the newer structures becoming superimposed on the old in the course of development. The more complex emergent organization must not only provide an effective means for discharge and control, but must also include systems of inhibition directed against the utilization of the older structures [p. 264].

In Sandler's view, then, regression is a disinhibition within the older structure rather than an actual reversal or backward movement to that structure. The notion of persistence continued to occupy a central position in Sandler's thinking. For example, in his presidential address to the International Psycho-Analytical Association Congress, Sandler (1993) pointed to primary identification that invariably characterizes interpersonal perceptions. If we observe someone stumbling off the curb, we automatically right ourselves, demonstrating the continued presence of primitive modes of thought that may be incorporated in the far more elaborate process of empathy.

In 1994, Sandler and Sandler extended the notion of persistence by applying the distinction between past and present unconscious to the phenomenon of regression. As observed clinically, regression (i.e., manifest regression) is not going back in time but, rather, relaxing an antiregressive role of the ego. This antiregressive function, which stops the individual working at a lower developmental level (using structures that have persisted through development), is central to the phenomenon of resistance in clinical psychoanalysis. Thus, psychoanalysis may be seen as enabling the patient to relax antiregressive functioning in the service of the analysis. Allowing oneself to consciously tolerate previously intolerable unconscious wishes, positions one to find better solutions or compromises to conflicts between wishful fantasies and defensive self-protective motives. Thus, benign regression or controlled relaxation of the antiregression function is a central agent of therapeutic change.

Contribution to Epistemology

Almost all of Sandler's contributions could be regarded as epistemological contributions. His overarching aim appears to have been to divest psychoanalysis of conceptual confusions, circularity, and reification. The pattern of his writing has been to explore the history of a term or concept in psychoanalysis, then to elaborate on the multiple and frequently mutually incompatible meanings attached to the term. Having analyzed the historical changes in terminology, he explains how misconceptions emerged or discussions at different levels of abstraction were conflated. Then, with a minimal number of assumptions, he proposes a highly economical model that encompasses the multiple uses of the varying meanings of the construct under scrutiny. A good example of this approach is his paper with Christopher Dare on the psychoanalytic concept of orality (Sandler and Dare, 1970).

Perhaps it was Sandler's experience in the Hampstead Clinic, as well as his intellectual evolution in the theoretical turmoil of the British Psychoanalytic Society, that led him to the important insight that much of psychoanalytic theoretical development is preceded by the unconsciously constructed partial theories that evolve in the minds of practicing experienced analysts as they struggle to develop mental models of the minds of their patients. In his oft-cited paper on the relations between concept and practice in psychoanalysis (Sandler, 1983), he pointed to the necessity for such prototheories, as well as the simultaneous presence of incompatible preconscious theoretical constructions in the minds of many analysts. Evidence for such heterogeneity in the mental models of analysts may be found readily in the multiplicity of uses of psychoanalytic concepts, whose meaning cannot be derived without also considering their clinical context. The correspondence between "official theory" and such tentative intuitions determines the likelihood of their emergence in consciousness. Sandler's contribution is a tribute to the tolerance of ambiguity required of theoreticians like him who make essential contributions by explicating these ideas which, however generally held, remain inaccessible to most of us.

Sandler was one of an unfortunately small number of psychoanalysts fully committed to the importance of research that complements clinical work. Fundamentally, he was an empiricist. He saw psychoanalytic theory as a frame of reference to be applied to observations "be it in diagnosis, therapy, education, or research" (Sandler, 1960b, p. 128; Sandler, 1962). He recognized the role of settings other than the consulting room as a way to test psychoanalytic assumptions: "psychoanalysts are constantly making psychological assumptions, and whatever light can be thrown on these assumptions, whether in the consulting room or the laboratory, must be of immense value" (Sandler, 1960b, p. 150).

Conclusion

Sandler developed a psychology of feelings, internal representations, and adaptation closely tied to the behaviors of the analytic couple in the analytic situation. Besides contributing to our changing views of psychoanalytic theory, he also influenced psychoanalytic technique. His concept of role responsiveness was consistent with his view that the internal world involves internal representations of self and object, the actions between them, and the affects carried by those actions. The "three-box" model of psychic structure, emphasizing the importance of distinguishing the present from the past unconscious, led to the fruitful reexamination of further metapsychological and clinical concepts, including transference and countertransference. Finally, Sandler was instrumental in forming a dedicated cadre of analytic researchers whose contributions were beginning to influence analytic ideas. He was a bridging force in psychoanalysis, attempting to find the inherent linkages between apparently opposing ideas, and helping to close the gap between American ego psychologists and British Kleinian and object relations theorists. Perhaps a more radical appraisal of his involvement would attribute to him the preparation of the theoretical groundwork for the emergence of psychoanalytic relational theory.

No evaluation of Joseph Sandler's contribution would be complete without mention of Anne-Marie, his wife. Of course, many of the key papers were coauthored with her including the "three-box" model (Sandler and Sandler, 1983), the book on object relations (Sandler and Sandler, 1998), the memory paper (Sandler and Sandler, 1997), and so on. The caricature depiction of their partnership as theoretician (JS) and clinician (AMS) is actually very far from the truth. Both of them were firmly grounded in both practice and theory. Anne-Marie contributed both the deeply developmental timbre of their object relations model and the humanist, almost relational, highly transference-focused perspective that her clinical work well represents. Her perspective, colored by her background as a student of Jean Piaget and her continued enthusiasm for child analysis, added a realism to the developmental speculations and a groundedness in the description of interpersonal encounters that is relatively rare in psychoanalytic writings.

Joseph Sandler was a quiet revolutionary, yet revolutionary nevertheless. At the beginning of his career, psychoanalysis was dominated by an untenable mechanistic theory of affects, relationships, and clinical work. By systematizing available knowledge and scrutinizing this in relation to clinical observations, Sandler derived a new model that appeared to those working with him to be little more than a coherent restatement of existing ideas. However, moving psychoanalysis to the level of representation and reconceptualizing motivation as organized by a desire for safety, rather than anxiety or tension reduction, created a profoundly different environment for developments of theory and practice. In particular, understanding current relationships, however confusing, maladaptive, or perverse, as motivated by the experience of safety that such a relationship pattern can yield, has permitted consideration of the actual relationship that exists between patient and analyst as the primary organizer of therapeutic thinking. This breakthrough brought the majority of psychoanalytic schools together on the same intellectual platform for the first time since the death of Freud. Suddenly there was room for Kleinian ideas of projective identification, British Independent ideas of the holding environment, North American object relations concepts as well as self-psychological ones. Perhaps with the important exception of French psychoanalysis, object relations theory as formulated by Sandler could provide a common pathway for Anglo-Saxon psychoanalysis. An indication of his success is that Sandler is perhaps the only psychoanalyst to be regularly cited by both British Kleinian and North American Freudian authors, as well as all other groups. The current psychoanalytic revolution, which brought the Sullivanian interpersonalist approach back into the psychoanalytic limelight, would be inconceivable without the preparatory work brought about by Sandler's shift of emphasis from drive to affect, from ego and external world to self and object, and from repressed childhood experience to the present unconscious. Sandler has been the conduit from the residues of early 20th-century psychoanalysis to psychoanalysis of the 21st century. He deserves our gratitude, not simply for his own massive intellectual contributions, but also for the possibility he created for all of us to make our own.

REFERENCES

Blatt, S. J. & Behrends, R. S. (1987), Internalization, separation-individuation, and the nature of therapeutic action. *Internat. J. Psycho-Anal.*, 68:279–297.

Bowlby, J. (1973), *Attachment and Loss, Vol. 2.* London: Hogarth Press.

_______ (1980), *Attachment and Loss, Vol. 3.* London: Hogarth Press.

Cavell, M. (1994), *The Psychoanalytic Mind.* Cambridge, MA: Harvard University Press.

Davidson, D. (1980), *Actions, Reasons, and Causes: Essays on Action and Events*. Oxford, England: Clarendon Press.

Emde, R. N. (1980a), Toward a psychoanalytic theory of affect, Part 1: The organizational model and its propositions. In: *The Course of Life: Infancy and Early Childhood,* ed. S. I. Greenspan & G. H. Pollock. Washington, DC: DHSS, pp. 63–83.

_______ (1980b), Toward a psychoanalytic theory of affect, Part 2: Emerging models of emotional development in infancy. In: *The Course of Life: Infancy and Early Childhood,* ed. S. I. Greenspan & G. H. Pollock. Washington, DC: DHSS, pp. 85–112.

_______ (1988), Development terminable and interminable II: Recent psychoanalytic theory and therapeutic considerations. *Internat. J. Psycho-Anal.,* 69:283–286.

Fonagy, P., Gergely, G., Jurist, E. & Target, M. (2002), *Affect Regulation, Mentalization and the Development of the Self*. New York: Other Press.

Fraiberg, S. H., Adelson, E. & Shapiro, V. (1975), Ghosts in the nursery: A psychoanalytic approach to the problem of impaired infant–mother relationships. *J. Amer. Acad. Child Psychiat.,* 14:387–422.

Freud, S. (1900), The interpretation of dreams. *Standard Edition,* 4 & 5. London: Hogarth Press, 1953.

_______ (1933), New introductory lectures on psychoanalysis. *Standard Edition,* 22:1–182. London: Hogarth Press, 1964.

Gardner, H. (1985), *The Mind's Best Work*. New York: Basic Books.

Greenberg, J. R. & Mitchell, S. A. (1983), *Object Relations in Psychoanalytic Theory*. Cambridge, MA: Harvard University Press.

Head, H. (1926), *Aphasia and Kindred Disorders of Speech*. New York: Macmillan.

Hermann, I. (1923), Zur Psychologie der Chimpanzen. *Internat. Zeitschr. Psychoanal.,* 9:80–87.

Horowitz, M. J. (1991), Person schemas. In: *Person Schemas and Maladaptive Interpersonal Patterns,* ed. M. J. Horowitz. Chicago: University of Chicago Press, pp. 13–31.

Jacobson, E. (1953a), The affects and their pleasure–unpleasure qualities in relation to the psychic discharge processes. In: *Affects, Drives, Behavior,* ed. R. Loewenstein. New York: International Universities Press, pp. 38–66.

_______ (1953b), Contribution to the metapsychology of cyclothymic depression. In: *Affective Disorders: Psychoanalytic Contributions to Their Study,* ed. P. Greenacre. New York: International Universities Press, pp. 49–83.

_______ (1954a), Contribution to the metapsychology of psychotic identifications. *J. Amer. Psychoanal. Assn.,* 2:239–262.

_______ (1954b), On psychotic identifications. *Internat. J. Psycho-Anal.,* 35:102–108.

_______ (1954c), The self and the object world: Vicissitudes of their infantile cathexes and their influence on ideational affective development. *The Psychoanalytic Study of the Child,* 9:75–127. New York: International Universities Press.

_______ (1964), *The Self and the Object World*. New York: International Universities Press.

Joffe, W. G. & Sandler, J. (1965), Notes on pain, depression, and individuation. *The Psychoanalytic Study of the Child,* 20:394–424. New York: International Universities Press.

_______ & _______ (1968), Comments on the psychoanalytic psychology of adaptation, with special reference to the role of affects and the representational world. *Internat. J. Psycho-Anal.,* 49:445–454.

Kernberg, O. F. (1975), *Borderline Conditions and Pathological Narcissism.* New York: Aronson.

_______ (1976), *Object Relations Theory and Clinical Psychoanalysis.* New York: Aronson.

Klein, M. (1927), Symposium on child analysis. In: *Love, Guilt and Reparation: The Writings of Melanie Klein, Vol. 1.* London: Hogarth Press, 1975, pp. 139–169.

_______ (1933), The early development of conscience in the child. In: *Contributions to Psycho-Analysis, 1921–1945,* ed. M. Klein. London: Hogarth Press, 1948.

_______ (1958), On the development of mental functioning. In: *The Writings of Melanie Klein, Vol. 3: Envy and Gratitude and Other Works.* London: Hogarth Press, 1975, pp. 236–246.

Masterson, J. F. (1985), *The Real Self: A Developmental, Self, and Object Relations Approach.* New York: Brunner/Mazel.

Ogden, T. H. (1992), The dialectically constituted/decentred subject of psychoanalysis, II: The contributions of Klein and Winnicott. *Internat. J. Psycho-Anal.,* 73:613–626.

Peterfreund, E. (1971), *Information, Systems, and Psychoanalysis: An Evolutionary Biological Approach to Psychoanalytic Theory.* New York: International Universities Press.

Piaget, J. (1936), *The Origins of Intelligence in Children.* New York: International Universities Press, 1952.

_______ (1937), *The Construction of Reality in the Child.* New York: Basic Books, 1954.

Rosenblatt, A. D. & Thickstun, J. T. (1970), A study of the concept of psychic energy. *Internat. J. Psycho-Anal.,* 51:265–278.

_______ & _______ (1977), *Modern Psychoanalytic Concepts in a General Psychology, Part 1: General Concepts and Principles; Part 2: Motivation.* New York: International Universities Press.

Sandler, J. (1960a), The background of safety. *Internat. J. Psycho-Anal.,* 41:191–198.

_______ (1960b), On the concept of superego. *The Psychoanalytic Study of the Child,* 15:128–162. New York: International Universities Press.

_______ (1962), Psychology and psychoanalysis. *Brit. J. Med. Psychol.,* 35:91–100.

_______ (1967), Trauma, strain, and development. In: *Psychic Trauma,* ed. S. S. Furst. New York: Basic Books.

_______ (1972), The role of affects in psychoanalytic theory. In: *From Safety to Superego: Selected Papers of Joseph Sandler,* ed. J. Sandler. New York: Guilford Press, pp. 285–300.

_______ (1974), Psychological conflict and the structural model: Some clinical and theoretical implications. *Internat. J. Psycho-Anal.,* 55:53–72.

_______ (1975), Sexual fantasies and sexual theories in childhood. In: *Studies in Child Psychoanalysis: Pure and Applied.* New York: International Universities Press.

_______ (1976a), Countertransference and role responsiveness. *Internat. Rev. Psycho-Anal.,* 3:43–47.

_______ (1976b), Dreams, unconscious phantasies, and "identity of perception." *Internat. Rev. Psycho-Anal.*, 3:33–42.

_______ (1981), Character traits and object relationships. *Psychoanal. Quart.*, 50: 694–708.

_______ (1983), Reflections on some relations between psychoanalytic concepts and psychoanalytic practice. *Internat. J. Psycho-Anal.*, 64:35–45.

_______ (1987), The concept of projective identification. In: *Projection, Identification, Projection Identification,* ed. J. Sandler. Madison, CT: International Universities Press, pp. 13–26.

_______ (1989), Toward a reconsideration of the psychoanalytic theory of motivation. In: *Psychoanalysis: Toward the Second Century,* ed. A. M. Cooper, O. F. Kernberg & E. S. Person. New Haven, CT: Yale University Press, pp. 91–110.

_______ (1990), On the structure of internal objects and internal object relationships. *Psychoanal. Inq.*, 10:163–181.

_______ (1993), From listening to interpretation. *Internat. J. Psycho-Anal.*, 74:1097–1107.

_______ (1994), Fantasy, defense, and the representational world. *Infant Ment. Health J.*, 15:26–35.

_______ (1995), On attachment to internal objects. Presented at conference "Clinical Implications of Attachment: The Work of Mary Main," University College London.

_______ & Dare, C. (1970), The psychoanalytic concept of orality. *J. Psychosom. Res.*, 14:211–222.

_______ _______ & Holder, A. (1972a), Frames of reference in psychoanalytic psychology, I: Introduction. *Brit. J. Med. Psychol.*, 45:127–132.

_______ _______ & _______ (1972b), Frames of reference in psychoanalytic psychology, III: A note on the basic assumptions. *Brit. J. Med. Psychol.*, 45:143–148.

_______ _______ & _______ (1973), *The Patient and the Analyst: The Basis of the Psychoanalytic Process*. New York: International Universities Press.

_______ _______ & _______ (1974), Frames of reference in psychoanalytic psychology, VIII: The topographical frame of reference: Transference as an illustration of the functioning of the mental apparatus. *Brit. J. Med. Psychol.*, 47:43–51.

_______ _______ & _______ (1978), Frames of reference in psychoanalytic psychology, XI: Limitations of the topographical model. *Brit. J. Med. Psychol.*, 51:61–65.

_______ _______ & _______ (1982), Frames of reference in psychoanalytic psychology, XII: The characteristics of the structural frame of reference. *Brit. J. Med. Psychol.*, 55:203–207.

_______ Holder, A. & Dare, C. (1972), Frames of reference in psychoanalytic psychology, VI: The affect-trauma frame of reference. *Brit. J. Med. Psychol.*, 45:265–272.

_______ _______ & _______ (1973a), Frames of reference in psychoanalytic psychology, V: The topographical frame of reference: The organization of the mental apparatus. *Brit. J. Med. Psychol.*, 46:29–36.

_______ _______ & _______ (1973b), Frames of reference in psychoanalytic psychology, VII: The topographical frame of reference: The preconscious and the conscious. *Brit. J. Med. Psychol.*, 46:143–153.

_______ _______ & _______ (1973c), Frames of reference in psychoanalytic psychology, VI: The topographical frame of reference: The unconscious. *Brit. J. Med. Psychol.*, 46:37–43.

_______ _______ & _______ (1975), Frames of reference in psychoanalytic psychology, IX: Dream processes in the topographical frame of reference. *Brit. J. Med. Psychol.,* 48:161–174.

_______ _______ & _______ (1976), Frames of reference in psychoanalytic psychology, X: Narcissism and object-love in the second phase of psychoanalysis. *Brit. J. Med. Psychol.,* 49:267–274.

_______ _______ Kawenoka, M., Kennedy, H. & Neurath, L. (1969), Notes on some theoretical and clinical aspects of transference. *Internat. J. Psycho-Anal.,* 50: 633–645.

_______ _______ & Meers, D. (1963), The ego ideal and the ideal self. *The Psychoanalytic Study of the Child,* 18:139–158. New York: International Universities Press.

_______ & Joffe, W. G. (1965a), Notes on childhood depression. *Internat. J. Psycho-Anal.,* 46:88–96.

_______ & _______ (1965b), Notes on obsessional manifestations in children. *The Psychoanalytic Study of the Child,* 20:425–438. New York: International Universities Press.

_______ & _______ (1967), The tendency to persistence in psychological function and development with special reference to fixation and regression. *Bull. Menn. Clin.,* 31:257–271.

_______ & _______ (1969), Towards a basic psychoanalytic model. *Internat. J. Psycho-Anal.,* 50:79–90.

_______ & Nagera, H. (1963), Aspects of the metapsychology of fantasy. *The Psychoanalytic Study of the Child,* 18:159–194. New York: International Universities Press.

_______ & Rosenblatt, B. (1962), The concept of the representational world. *The Psychoanalytic Study of the Child,* 17:128–145. New York: International Universities Press.

_______ & Sandler, A.-M. (1978), On the development of object relationships and affects. *Internat. J. Psycho-Anal.,* 59:285–296.

_______ & _______ (1983), The "second censorship," the "three-box model," and some technical implications. *Internat. J. Psycho-Anal.,* 64:413–426.

_______ & _______ (1984), The past unconscious, the present unconscious, and interpretation of the transference. *Psychoanal. Inq.,* 4:367–399.

_______ & _______ (1986), The gyroscopic function of unconscious fantasy. In: *Towards a Comprehensive Model for Schizophrenic Disorders,* ed. D. B. Feinsilver. New York: Analytic Press, pp. 109–123.

_______ & _______ (1987), The past unconscious, the present unconscious, and the vicissitudes of guilt. *Internat. J. Psycho-Anal.,* 68:331–341.

_______ & _______ (1994), Theoretical and technical comments on regression and anti-regression. *Internat. J. Psycho-Anal.,* 75:431–439.

_______ & _______ (1997), A psychoanalytic theory of repression and the unconscious. In: *Recovered Memories of Abuse: True or False?* ed. J. Sandler & P. Fonagy. London: Karnac Books, pp. 163–181.

_______ & _______ (1998), *Object Relations Theory and Role Responsiveness.* London: Karnac Books.

Schafer, R. (1976), *A New Language for Psychoanalysis.* New Haven, CT: Yale University Press.

_______ (1978), *Language and Insight*. New Haven, CT: Yale University Press.
Spitz, R. (1965), *The First Year of Life*. New York: International Universities Press.
Stern, D. N. (1985), *The Interpersonal World of the Infant: A View from Psychoanalysis and Developmental Psychology*. New York: Basic Books.
Stolorow, R. D. & Atwood, G. E. (1979), *Faces in a Cloud: Subjectivity in Personality Theory*. New York: Aronson.
Westen, D. (1991), Social cognition and object relations. *Psycholog. Bull.,* 109: 429–455.
Winnicott, D. W. (1956), Mirror role of mother and family in child development. In: *Playing and Reality,* ed. D. W. Winnicott. London: Tavistock, pp. 111–118.

Sub-Department of Clinical Health Psychology
University College London
Gower Street
London WC1E 6BT
England
p.fonagy@ucl.ac.uk

A Contemporary View of Some of Joseph Sandler's Key Concepts

ALEX HOLDER, PH.D.

Three of Sandler's seminal papers—"The Background of Safety" (1960a), "The Concept of the Representational World" (1962), and "Countertransference and Role Responsiveness" (1976)—are scrutinized and discussed to explore the evolution of his thinking over some 40 years. His early insistence on the importance of feeling states and intrapsychic mechanisms and processes, especially those relating to internal objects and internal object relationships, are emphasized as well as the interactions and complementary relationship between theoretical formulations and clinical findings, as exemplified in his research activities in the Index Department of the Anna Freud Centre in London and in his paper on countertransference and role responsiveness. Interrelationships with other concepts, both clinical and theoretical, show up in Sandler's work as well as that of other eminent authors up to the present time, and similarities in conceptualizations are highlighted. Sandler's continuous efforts to clarify psychoanalytic concepts and to integrate differing psychoanalytic conceptualizations and models are illustrated by references to and quotations from the salient papers.

JOSEPH SANDLER WAS A PROLIFIC WRITER. HE PUBLISHED WELL OVER 50 books and papers, some written on his own and many in collaboration

Alex Holder, Ph.D. is Training and Supervising Analyst, German Psychoanalytical Association; since 1998, he has been Editor, *International Psychoanalysis,* news magazine of the International Psychoanalytical Association.

with colleagues, especially during the years when he was in charge of the Index Department at the Hampstead Clinic, now the Anna Freud Centre, in London. It cannot have been an easy task for the Editor of this issue of *Psychoanalytic Inquiry* to select just three papers containing some of Sandler's key concepts. I think his choice has been very felicitous, starting with the early paper on "The Background of Safety" (1960a), which already reflects the central importance that feeling states always had for Sandler. "The Concept of the Representational World" (1962), written jointly with Bernard Rosenblatt, and one of the results of the research work in the Index Department, has become something of a classic and already foreshadows the links of ego psychology with the later object relations theories, in particular the notions of the "internal object" and "internal object relationships." And the much later paper, "Countertransference and Role Responsiveness" (1976), highlights the application of theoretical conceptualizations to clinical work, and vice versa.

Having had the privilege of working closely with Joe Sandler for many years (Sandler, Holder, and Meers, 1963; Sandler et al., 1992; Sandler et al., 1997), both in the Index Department of the Anna Freud Centre and at the Maudsley Hospital in London, I know what a creative thinker he was and how important it was for him to ensure that psychoanalytical theories always matched clinical observations and that theoretical notions had to be modified if clinical findings contradicted them. The rich clinical data collected in the Hampstead Index were a treasure trove for research into psychoanalytical concepts and the starting point for many research projects culminating in a wealth of papers, of which "The Concept of the Representational World" is one of the earliest.

"The Background of Safety" (1960)

The recognition of the centrality of affects as motivators and regulators of psychic functioning and behavior has become more pronounced in the course of the history and development of psychoanalysis, in particular the emphasis and focus on the crucial importance of an infant's earliest affective experiences in relating to its emotionally most important objects. Sandler was one of the first to recognize and conceptualize this, and in elevating the infant's basic need to feel safe to a "safety principle," he was daring enough to place it side by side with Freud's pleasure and reality principles: "I want to put forward . . . the notion of a *safety-principle* which mediates the development of the reality-principle from the pleasure-principle" (1960a, p. 352). Fonagy, Cooper, and Wallerstein (1999), in their chapter "Joseph Sandler's Intellectual Contributions to Theoretical and Clinical Psychoanalysis," call it a

> revolutionary concept that placed the operating principle of ego in a positive framework of trying to maximize safety or security rather than to avoid anxiety. Although Sandler recognized the inverse complementarity of anxiety and safety, he was able to show that the pursuit of safety is an overarching construct, compatible with instinct theory, that has the capacity to organize defenses, perceptions, and fantasies [p. 7].

Indeed, for Sandler (1960a), a decrease in anxiety automatically leads to an increase in safety feelings: "Such successful sensory integration is not only accompanied by anxiety reduction, but also contributes to a background feeling within the ego, a feeling which can be referred to as one of safety or perhaps security" (p. 353). In calling it a "background feeling," Sandler probably wanted to convey that such feelings need not be conscious at all but can operate at a descriptively unconscious level. They constitute an affective state which is associated with a "feeling of well-being" and thus are related to the regulation of self-esteem, another of Sandler's central notions. In his introductory note to the publication of this paper in *From Safety to Superego,* Sandler (1987) points out that the "introduction of the notion of safety as a feeling state, quite distinct from feelings of sensual pleasure, foreshadows the later emphasis on the part played by feelings of well-being in the regulation of mental functioning" (p. 1). With hindsight, Sandler adds another important point that extends the notion of safety beyond its link to perception to which it is restricted in the paper itself: "Although this paper makes use of the example of perception as an activity that can generate feelings of safety, it should be emphasized that *all* aspects of psychobiological functioning, insofar as they proceed smoothly and harmoniously, can be regarded as generating safety feeling" (p. 1).

This extension to all psychobiological functioning means, of course, that the range of sources that can provide a sense of safety or well-being is considerably greater than the earlier restriction to perception alone had been. This gives the individual much greater flexibility and more opportunities to establish or maintain feelings of safety and through them a state of relative well-being. Nevertheless, perception—and in particular the notion of "identity of perception"—has always played a central role in Sandler's thinking and conceptualizations. This is discussed at greater length later in this essay.

Another important point to which Sandler (1990a) draws attention in a much later paper is that the content of the wishes involved in a fantasied internal relationship between the self and an object need not always be an instinctual drive wish, "but includes wishes to maintain well-being, safety, and feelings of being in control. Moreover, a powerful motivating force is the need to defend against unpleasant feelings or against the anticipation of such feelings. And there is a constant pressure to replenish supplies of well-being, security, and self-esteem" (p. 164). "Fantasied internal relationships" hardly had any place in Sandler's early paper on feelings of safety. He was still more interested then in the actual interactions between the infant/child and caretakers, and in the repercussions that this had on the feeling states generated by the infant. As we shall see later, Sandler gradually shifted his focus to the proliferation of fantasies with which object representations, as well as the self-representation, are invested in the course of development, and how defensive needs play an important role in this attempt to secure a sufficient sense of safety and well-being.

Although Sandler (1960a) conceptualizes the feeling of safety as the "polar opposite" (p. 353) of anxiety, he also postulates parallel processes, such as those of "safety-signals" (p. 354), corresponding to Freud's notion of signal anxiety. Whereas signal anxiety alerts the ego to an impending internal danger (i.e., a conflict), safety-signals are an indication of a mental state that points in the direction of greater safety and leads to efforts to increase and maximize efforts in that direction. Sandler probably had something like this in mind when he speaks of a "technique for raising the level of safety-feeling" which consists in the "*hypercathexis* of certain sources of stimulation which lead to secure perceptions" (p. 355). One has to remember that for Sandler, the "act of perception is an act of ego-mastery through which the ego copes with the excitation, that is, with unorganized sense data, and is thus protected from being traumatically overwhelmed" and that the "successful act of perception is an act of integration which is accompanied by a definite *feeling of safety*" (p. 352). As Sandler points out later, it is traumata, dangers, and anxieties deriving from any source that threaten or obliterate the safety level or feeling (p. 354).

In the context of social violence, Gampel (1999) introduced the notion of the "background of the uncanny" (p. 59) in the case of individuals who have experienced man-made disasters or extreme social violence and has juxtaposed it to Sandler's background of safety. Whether, as Gampel maintains, both backgrounds exist in all of us and are active at different levels and at different moments (p. 62) remains an open question.

Sandler's juxtaposition of a "safety principle" with the pleasure principle (and its later transformation into the reality principle) suggests that he regarded it in the nature of an inborn tendency that becomes operative sometime after birth as a motivational driving force which overrides that of instinctual drive gratification. In this sense, Sandler's concept can be compared with Bowlby's notion of a "secure attachment" and Ainsworth's concept of a "secure base." However, for Bowlby (1988), attachment behavior was an innate given that comes into operation after birth. Thus, his attachment theory emphasizes the

> primary status and biological function of intimate emotional bonds between individuals, the maintaining of which are postulated to be controlled by a cybernetic system situated within the central nervous system, utilizing working models of self and attachment figure in relationship with each other [p. 120].

In contrast, Sandler's concept of the safety principle places the emphasis on the experiential in the infant's efforts to attain feelings of safety. However, since Sandler elevates this search to a "principle" and thus places it on a par with the pleasure principle, one could argue that, at least implicitly, he also had some inborn tendency in mind. On the other hand, Bowlby (1988), too, acknowledges the importance of the experiential in determining the type of attachment which an infant develops: "There is today impressive and mounting evidence that the pattern of attachment that an individual develops during the years of immaturity—infancy, childhood, and adolescence—is profoundly influenced by the way his parents . . . treat him" (pp. 123–124).

Emde (1988) has also emphasized the crucial importance of the positive emotional transactions between an infant and his caregiver in order to foster an intrapsychic climate that promotes growth and very much corresponds to Sandler's notion of the background of safety:

> Nowhere is the affective core of self more salient than in infancy. Emotional signaling between infant and caregiver provides the basis for communicating needs, intentions, and satisfactions. It communicates meaning and motivates. It provides a guide not only for need satisfaction but for learning, loving, and exploring. Indeed, it is emotional availability of the caregiver in infancy which seems to be the most central growth-promoting feature of the early rearing experience. Such a principle has been implicit in investigations of attachment . . . and has been made explicit as a clinical generalization by Mahler and her colleagues. . . . Experimental approaches are especially revealing. In one study of 15-month-olds, we found striking effects of mother's emotional availability on infant exploration and play, depending on whether mother was reading a newspaper or not (Sorce and Emde, 1981). In another set of experiments, we explored the importance of emotional signaling through a phenomenon we and others have called "social referencing" [p. 32].

In a more general way, Kernberg (1982) has elevated affects to the "primary motivational system, in the sense that they are at the center of each of the infinite number of gratifying and frustrating concrete events the infant experiences with his environment" (p. 907). For him, "affective behavior strongly influences object relations from birth on. . . . A central biological function of inborn affective patterns . . . is to signal to the environment (the mothering person) the infant's needs, and to thus initiate communication between the infant and mother and this marks the beginning of intrapsychic life" (p. 906). Whereas the object relations aspect is only implicit in Sandler's paper, it has become quite explicit in Kernberg's: "Affects, operating as the earliest motivational system, are therefore intimately linked with the fixation by memory of an internalized world of object relations" (p. 907). Furthermore, he bases his view of affects as being the primary motivational system on more recent neuropsychological theories pertaining to the "storage of affective memory in the limbic cortex" (p. 907).

In discussing the relationship between affects and instinctual drives (both libido and aggression), Kernberg postulates, "Affects, in short, are the building blocks or constituents of instinctual drives; affects eventually acquire a signal function for the activation of instinctual drives" (p. 908). In Sandler's view, the safety principle would be the supraordinate one in that it may inhibit the activation of instinctual drives if the safety-signal indicates that such activation would lead to an increase in anxiety.

It seems to me that Stern's (1985) concept of "affect attunement" has much to do with the generation and maintenance of safety feelings. Although Stern discusses affect attunement only in connection with "The Sense of a Subjective Self" (pp. 138ff.), it would seem that such affective attunement between mother and infant already is of central importance before the age of seven to nine months where Stern places the beginning of the sense of a subjective self. In this context, Stern speaks of "interaffectivity," which is what is mainly meant when one speaks of "mirroring" or "empathic responsiveness" on the part of a parent (p. 138). Surely, a good-enough mother is trying to respond in this way from earliest infancy onward. The successful and continuous sharing of affective states must greatly contribute to an infant's sense of safety and, conversely, threaten that sense if the affective dialogue between mother and infant is derailed.

When Stern enumerates the processes which must occur for an intersubjective affective exchange to take place, he describes some capacities on the part of the infant which are obviously not possible before seven to nine months of age. Nevertheless, something similar must happen before then to give the infant a sense of being understood and to feel safe. Stern, in fact, acknowledges this when he refers to a great number of studies that demonstrate "how caregivers and infants mutually create the chains and sequences of reciprocal behaviors that make up social dialogues during the infant's first nine months" (p. 139). Although this interaction occurs largely on an imitative basis, Stern points out that the mother already introduces "modifying imitations" during these earliest months or provides a "theme-and-variation format with slight changes in her contribution at each dialogic turn" (p. 139). Stern continues,

> When the infant is around nine months old, however, one begins to see the mother add a new dimension to her imitative behavior, a dimension that appears to be geared to the infant's new status as a potentially intersubjective partner. . . . She begins to expand her behavior beyond true imitation into a new category of behavior we will call *affect attunement* [p. 140].

This statement is not quite consistent with Stern's previous assumption that a mother already introduces modifications to her "true imitation" long before that. It therefore appears that the changes that occur around the age of nine months are chiefly a consequence of a new developmental acquisition on the part of the infant which Stern describes as the third of three processes that must take place for what he calls an "intersubjective exchange of affect" to occur:

> First, the parent must be able to read the infant's feeling state from the infant's overt behavior. Second, the parent must perform some behavior that is not a strict imitation but nonetheless corresponds in some way to the infant's overt behavior. Third, the infant must be able to read this corresponding parental response as having to do with the infant's own original feeling experience and not just imitating the infant's behavior. It is only in the presence of these three conditions that feeling states within one person can be knowable to another and that they can both sense, without using language, that the transaction has occurred [p. 139].

What Stern (1985) describes here as the third process on the part of the infant seems to be based on an ability that Fonagy and Target (2000) conceptualized as "mentalization" and that they define as follows:

> Mentalization or reflective function is the developmental acquisition that permits children to respond not only to another person's behavior, but also to the child's conception of others' attitudes, intentions, or plans. Mentalization enables children to "read" other people's minds. By attributing mental states to

> others, children make people's behavior meaningful and predictable. . . . Exploring the meaning of others' actions, in turn, is crucially linked with the child's ability to label and find meaningful his own psychic experiences, an ability that we suggest underlies affect regulation, impulse control, self-monitoring, and the experience of self-agency [p. 132].

It seems that with the acquisition of this function, children also become better able to regulate their feelings of safety.

These selective examples from the more recent literature on the central importance of affects and feeling states in regulating mental functioning seem to confirm the basic ideas presented by Sandler (1960) in his paper on the background feeling of safety. These later papers enlarge Sandler's conceptualization to affects in general and they also emphasize the crucial importance of the earliest affective interchanges between caregiver and infant.

One of the most innovative ideas in Sandler's (1960) paper is the notion that human beings sometimes cling to painful states precisely because they feel safety from them. This is particularly striking in psychotic manifestations:

> These can, in part at any rate, be understood as attempts to raise the safety-feeling level by gaining a secure source of stable perceptions which correspond to intact object-, thing-, or movement-representations within the fragmented psychotic ego. These perceptions result in an increase in the level of safety feeling, through a hypercathexis of the residual but secure perception [p. 355].

In a much later paper, Sandler (1990b) returns to this apparent paradox, now discussing it from the point of view of intrapsychic "dialogues" between the self and an object, which, although painful, provide the person with a feeling of safety since they allow for the continued presence of the safety-giving object in fantasy. Referring to Weiss's notion of internal psychic "presences" and Schafer's "primary-process presences," Sandler states:

> Even if the presences in fantasy are persecuting, guilt-making ones, they nevertheless have the function of carrying the

> individual's own projected aggression while at the same time providing a background feeling of safety. It is worth reminding ourselves here of the way in which battered children resist separation from their parents; in the same way, a need is fulfilled by the existence of "battering" internal objects and their reflections in unconscious fantasy [p. 874].

"The Concept of the Representational World" (1962)

In their introductory chapter to *Psychoanalysis on the Move: The Work of Joseph Sandler,* Fonagy and colleagues (1999) state:

> It is evident to all serious scholars that [Sandler's] meticulous, systematic development of the representational-world framework, as introduced by Jacobson (1954) in her paper on "Self and the Object World," was the bedrock of the "quiet revolution" of psychoanalytic thought over the past quarter of a century [p. 4].

Indeed, it is a seminal paper still firmly rooted in Freud's structural model of the mind and, as Sandler (1962) noted elsewhere, an "auxiliary way of looking at things, of pulling parts of the psychoanalytical model together" (p. 98). Or the representational-world framework is a

> useful supplementary frame of reference to both the topographical and structural theories of the mind and was in no way intended to replace these theories. The representational approach has proved particularly useful as a basis for the further theoretical and clinical understanding of object relationships and of mechanisms of internalization and externalization [Sandler, 1987, p. 58].

A central concept of object relations theories is that of the "internal object," a term that may conjure up rather concrete connotations about a person inside one's psyche. It is one of the merits of Sandler's and Rosenblatt's (1962) paper that they spell out so clearly that we have to think of *representations* of objects—as well as of the representation of the self—which are built up gradually in the course of development, and that all these representations eventually have an enduring basic structure—they call them "stable object representations" (p. 132)—within which a whole range of different "shapes" or "images" can be distinguished.

> A representation can be considered to have a more or less enduring existence as an organization or schema which is constructed out of a multitude of impressions. A child experiences many images of his mother—mother feeding, mother talking, mother sitting down, mother standing up, mother preparing food, etc.—and on the basis of these gradually creates a mother representation that encompasses a whole range of mother images, all of which bear the label "mother" [p. 132].

Similarly, the self-representation has a great many shapes, as do the representations of other objects. Furthermore, every representation, in particular that of the self, has both conscious and unconscious aspects. It is again noteworthy that the emphasis, in this early paper, is on the object representations that evolve largely on the basis of experiences with real objects. The distortions of such representations by fantasies and by defense mechanisms (in particular projections and projective identifications) are not yet given the prominence which they receive in Sandler's later publications.

For instance, in a much later paper, Sandler (1990a) returns to the subject of internal objects and internal object relationships. He now takes the view—an extension of his earlier formulations—that internal objects have the "capacity to create, through the fantasy life of the individual, a quality of 'presence' of the object. The feeling of presence embodied in the fantasy figures derived from internal objects is a vital element in development and in the maintenance of a sense of autonomy and separateness from external objects" (p. 170). On the other hand, Sandler (1987) takes issue with a tendency, sometimes found in Kleinian literature, to describe intrapsychic mechanisms such as projections or projective identifications as though they were concrete happenings instead of displacements in fantasy from one representation to another. In this context, he quotes Bion, who speaks of the "evacuation of the bad breast [which] takes place through a realistic projective identification." Sandler feels that what Bion describes here "is a concrete 'putting into the object'" (p. 19). It all hinges, I suppose, on what Bion means by a *realistic* projective identification.

For Sandler and Rosenblatt (1962), the buildup of the representational world is clearly a function of the ego in its structural meaning: "The construction of a representational world is one of the functions of the ego" (p. 133). It is based on the way an infant or child (and, for that matter, also adults) perceives objects in the external world and then internalizes such perceptions as mental representations. These are primitive to begin with, are initially made up of part-object representations but become increasingly more complex as development proceeds.

> We know that perception is an *active* process . . . by means of which the ego transforms raw sensory data into meaningful percepts. From this it follows that the child creates, within its perceptual or *representational* world, images, and organizations of his internal as well as external environment. It is well known that the infant constantly confuses aspects of what we as *observers* would describe as "internal" and "external" reality within its representational world [pp. 131–132].

Whereas Sandler and Rosenblatt clearly emphasized experiential elements in the buildup of the representational world, the Kleinian view of the genesis of internal objects stressed the contribution of primitive unconscious fantasies which tend to distort the experiential aspects of the interactions with objects. Sandler has always remained very critical of such conceptualizations. In a much later joint paper with Anne-Marie Sandler (1978), we read:

> In their [Klein and her followers'] formulations, they appear to have attributed profound psychological knowledge to the infant by confounding psychological and biological behavior. As a consequence they endow the infant with psychological intentionality and complex cognition in the first weeks of life. In our view, the infant is, for a considerable time, the passive experiencer of his own activities, feelings and sensations. The capacity to create and manipulate fantasies and thoughts will, in our view, occur well after the first months of life [p. 285, fn.].

In other words, Sandler questions the inborn existence of fantasies that become operative from birth onward and shape the representations of internal objects.

Sandler and Rosenblatt's (1962) conceptualization of the representational world, however, is not restricted to living objects: "A specialized part of the representational world consists of symbols for things, activities, and relationships, and provides the furniture for the ego function of thinking" (p. 133). Furthermore, it includes the child's body representation and, in regard to the instinctual drives, "need and affect representations" (p. 133). Thus the representational world contains all the elements necessary for what Freud called "trial action in thought." It is therefore very apt for Sandler and Rosenblatt to compare the representational world to a stage in a theater where such trial actions can be imagined to occur.

> The characters on the stage represent the child's various objects, as well as the child himself. Needless to say, the child is usually the hero of the piece. The theater, which contains the stage, would correspond to aspects of the ego, and the various functions such as scene shifting, raising or lowering the curtain, and all the machinery auxiliary to the actual stage production would correspond to those ego functions of which we are not normally aware [p. 134].

Staying within this theater metaphor, we can think of signal anxiety, for instance, as part of the "auxiliary machinery," bringing such a trial action to an end if it is experienced as being too dangerous in its consequences, and setting in motion one of the defense mechanisms at the ego's disposal. Such mechanisms operate at a descriptively unconscious level. What can be seen is the end result—for example, a changed scene, a blackout, or a lowered curtain. What happens before on the stage is the imagined interaction between a particular "shape" of the self-representation (e.g., an instinctual drive wish that demands gratification) with a specific shape of an object representation. If the "staged" satisfaction of a particular wish arouses conflict, then the curtain may come down; that is, the repression barrier may come into operation. The ego can, of course, resort to other defense mechanisms at its disposal in order to deal with the anxiety generated by conflicts.

In another paper on internal object relationships, Sandler (1990b) applies a similar metaphor to the treatment situation when he states,

"In the analytic situation the patient unpacks the object aspects of his mental furniture, so to speak, and tries to position this furniture in ways that make it seem as if it belongs and is appropriate" (p. 878). It may at first seem to contradict his statements from the paper on the representational world in which he allocates the "object aspects" to the "mental furniture"—that is, to the nonexperiential realm of mental structures, mechanisms, and functions. But Sandler's thinking on internal objects and internal object relationships had progressed considerably between 1962 and 1990. It is above all the "crucial distinction" between the experiential and the nonexperiential realms which—as Sandler (1990b) then pointed out—"we failed to make sufficiently in the original work on the representational world" (p. 869). In "Toward a Basic Psychoanalytic Model," Sandler and Joffe (1969) drew attention to this distinction between the experiential and nonexperiential when they proposed that

> a sharp distinction be made between . . . the "experiential" and the "nonexperiential" realms. The realm of subjective experience . . . refers to the experience of the phenomenal content of wishes, impulses, memories, fantasies, sensations, percepts, feelings, and the like . . . experiential content of any sort, including feelings, *can be either conscious or unconscious*. . . . In sharp contrast is the "nonexperiential realm." This is the realm of forces and energies; of mechanisms and apparatuses; of organized structures, both biological and psychological; of sense organs and means of discharge. The nonexperiential realm is intrinsically unknowable, except insofar as it can become known through subjective experience [p. 241].

In his later paper, Sandler (1990b) allocated the internal object "to the psychological *structures* that lie outside the realm of subjective experience" and suggests "not to use the term for conscious or unconscious self- and object *images*" (p. 871). He elaborates that this view differs from that of the Kleinians for whom internal objects "are the objects experienced in unconscious fantasy . . . directly accessible to subjective experience." And he adds, "In this context the notion of *structure* is used in the sense of any enduring psychological organization, and *image* for subjective experience in any sensory modality" (p. 871).

In the 1962 paper, Sandler and Rosenblatt discuss the representational aspects of relationships between the self and an object primarily in terms of instinctual drive wishes which are directed toward an object for their satisfaction. They write,

> Needs soon become transformed *into wishes* of one sort or another in the course of development, and these wishes involve self- and object representations. Thus an unconscious wish, let us say, to exhibit one's body to another, involves the unconscious perception by the ego of an image of the object reacting in some way. These self- and object images must, it seems to us, be unconsciously appreciated by the ego and be dealt with in some way by it—for example, by repression (or some other form of defense) or by permitting an acceptable derivative to gain access to consciousness or motility. The distortion of the unconscious wish involves changes in the shape of the self- and object representations [pp. 135–136].

From a contemporary point of view, it seems obvious that the intrapsychic representations of object relationships are not solely determined by instinctual drive wishes. And if we think of Sandler's earlier paper on the background of safety, he himself acknowledged and asserted that safety feelings usually become supraordinate to the attainment of instinctual drive satisfaction. Thus it is, rather, the overall quality of the emotional relationship between an infant and his caregiver and its internalization as part of the representational world which is of crucial importance for growth and development. This point is made very strongly by Emde (1988) when he suggests,

> What may be formative about infancy experience is *not* that *infant* behavioral patterns get set in an enduring way, but rather that *infant–caregiver relationship* patterns get set up in an enduring way. Early relationship styles and patterns later become internalized by the individual in the progression from infancy to early childhood. . . . To put it another way, relationship aspects become internalized by the individual, continue as strong influences in development throughout childhood, and are activated in similar relationship contexts throughout life [p. 28].

Emde is putting forward this "new version of an old hypothesis" in the context of "behavioral genetics findings" that

> help make sense of the continuity paradox by pointing to developmental processes of change as well as continuity . . . the overriding importance of the specifically experienced (i.e., relationship) environment, and the special role of temperament and affectivity for individual differences in early development [p. 28].

In his later writings, Sandler, too, gives increasing importance to internal object relationships and attempts to actualize them in a real relationship, a subject I discuss next in the context of his paper "Countertransference and Role Responsiveness."

In Sandler's (1960b) discussion of certain other characteristics of the representational world, one can detect the seeds of ideas on which he elaborated in later papers. For instance, the development of "ideal selves" in order to obtain the "greatest narcissistic gain" (p. 136) and the question of primary versus secondary narcissism (p. 142) are taken up again at much greater length in the paper "The Ego Ideal and the Ideal Self," written jointly with Holder and Meers (1963), where a distinction is made between the "self-I-would-like-to-be" (the ideal self as part of the ego) and the "self-I-ought-to-be" (the ego ideal as part of the superego); or the more extensive discussion of the subject of fantasy—which, in the representational-world paper is regarded as the "purposive manipulation in imagination of the representational world" (p. 144)—in "Aspects of the Metapsychology of Fantasy," written jointly with Nagera (1963). On the other hand, the definition of introjection as the "vesting of certain object representations with a special status, so that these are felt to have all the authority and power of the real parents" (p. 138) draws on Sandler's (1960b) earlier paper "On the Concept of Superego."

"Countertransference and Role Responsiveness" (1976)

The two papers discussed so far—on the background of safety-feelings and the concept of the representational world—are essentially theoretical in nature, especially the latter, which arose from research carried out at the Anna Freud Centre. The paper to be discussed now is, as the title already suggests, the fruit of Sandler's clinical experiences. It is an impressive example of the interaction of theory and practice, an interdependence that was always of the utmost importance for Joe Sandler. The theoretical underpinning in this paper is Sandler's view that individuals, whether in analytic treatment or not, build up internal object relationships of a wishful nature which they attempt to actualize in a real relationship. This is precisely what also happens in the treatment situation where the analyst, in his countertransference, may feel manipulated by the patient. Quoting from *The Patient and the Analyst* (Sandler et al., 1992), we read: "transference need not be restricted to the illusory apperception of another person . . . but can be taken to include the unconscious (and often subtle) attempts to manipulate or provoke situations with others which are a concealed repetition of earlier experiences and relationships" (p. 43). Sandler continues,

> I believe such "manipulations" to be an important part of object relations in general, and to enter in "trial" form into the "scanning" of objects in the process of object choice. In the transference . . . the patient attempts to prod the analyst into behaving in a particular way. . . . I would make the link between certain countertransference responses and transference via the behavioral (verbal and nonverbal) *interaction* between the patient and the analyst [p. 44].

It is this interaction between patient and analyst for which Sandler has coined the term "role relationship," whereas the term "role responsiveness" addresses itself more specifically to processes that are set in motion in the analyst in response to the patient's verbal communications or behavior. For Sandler, this interaction is determined, to a large extent, by the

> intrapsychic role relationship which each party tries to impose on the other . . . from the side of the patient we may see a whole variety of very specific role relationships emerge . . . the role relationship of the patient in analysis at any particular time consists of a role in which he casts himself, and a *complementary*

> role in which he casts the analyst at that particular time . . . the patient, in the transference, attempts to *actualize these* [unconscious images or fantasies] *in a disguised way*" [p. 44].

Sandler uses here the notion of "actualizing" in the sense of "to make actual, to convert into an actual fact, to realize in action," as defined in the *Oxford English Dictionary.*

It is a real innovation when Sandler suggests a little later that, parallel to the famous and old-established "free-floating attention," the analyst should also adopt what he calls "free-floating responsiveness" (pp. 44–45). He continues,

> The analyst is, of course, not a machine in absolute self-control, only experiencing on the one hand, and delivering interpretations on the other, although much of the literature might seem to paint such a picture. Among many other things he talks, he greets the patient, he makes arrangements about practical matters, he may joke and, to some degree, allow his responses to depart from the classical psychoanalytic norm. My contention is that in the analyst's overt reactions to the patient as well as in his thoughts and feelings what can be called his "role responsiveness" shows itself, not only in his feelings but also in his attitudes and behavior, as a crucial element in his "useful" countertransference [p. 45].

While the "free-floating attention" is directed toward the verbal and nonverbal communications of the patient, the analyst's *free-floating responsiveness* is directed to the countertransference thoughts, fantasies, and feelings which that material evokes in the analyst's mind. In the context of his second clinical example, Sandler makes clear that the analyst can sometimes be prompted into a "free-floating behavioral responsiveness" (p. 47)—that is, when he enacts the role unconsciously forced on him by the patient.

When speaking about roles, Sandler returns to a metaphor that he and Rosenblatt already used in their paper on the representational world when they compared this world to a stage on which dramas are enacted. Schafer (1999) addressed himself to such enactments on the part of the analyst and suggested a similarity, if not correspondence, between Klein's concept of projective identification and Sandler's notion of role responsiveness: "the analyst's countertransference enactments have been attributed either to the analysand's projective identifications (a Kleinian emphasis) or to what Sandler (1976) called role responsiveness, regarded as the analyst's participation in 'actualizing' unconscious fantasies" (p. 77). However, Schafer continues to make the point that

> we cannot . . . fix "enactment" in one place forever. It is not possible to establish permanently the meaning of any psychoanalytic term. . . . Meanings evolve in psychoanalysis as they do in law: terms take on meaning as they are processed and decisions rendered; to begin with, they are virtually empty vessels waiting to be filled and refilled by a more or less changing history of usage and challenge [p. 77].

In *Projection, Identification, Projective Identification,* a book edited by Sandler (1989), he himself wrote the chapter on projective identification, in which he distinguishes three successive historical stages in the use of the concept, from Melanie Klein's introduction of the term through its extension by Heimann and Racker to the transference–countertransference relation between patient and analyst, to, finally, Bion's further extension in his notion of the analyst as a "container." Referring to Racker's distinction between concordant and complementary identifications on the part of the analyst in his countertransference, Sandler points out that "countertransference based on a concordant identification occurs when the analyst identifies with the patient's own fantasy self-representation of the moment. Countertransference based on a complementary identification occurs when the analyst identifies with the object representation in the patient's transference fantasy" (p. 18). Sandler goes on to summarize,

> Projective identification occurring within the person's fantasy life (reflected in a fantasy distortion of the analyst) can be called first-stage projective identification. If either the self or the object represented in such unconscious fantasies is identified with by the analyst to a degree sufficient to contribute to the analyst's countertransference, we have an instance of second-stage projective identification [p. 18].

It seems to me that Sandler, in the above quotation, makes an important point about the mechanism of projective identification. Initially, projective identification is a process or mechanism that occurs within a person's (unconscious) fantasy life; that is, it affects the self-representation and that of a specific object. If that person happens to be a patient in psychoanalytic treatment, the secondary effect of projective identification may be reflected in the transference in a fantasy distortion of the analyst. It is then this fantasy relationship to the analyst that the patient attempts to actualize in the treatment situation, with the analyst—ideally—becoming aware of this (unconscious) manipulation in his or her countertransference.

The two clinical examples that Sandler gives in his 1976 paper as illustrations of his thesis show how the analyst sometimes assumes the role unconsciously assigned to him by a patient, and it may indeed take him quite a while before understanding *that* he is enacting and *what* he is enacting or is enabling the patient to actualize. In this context, Sandler makes another important point when he emphasizes that an analyst's "irrational response" should not always automatically be regarded as due to a blind spot of his, but that, instead, it "may sometimes be usefully regarded as a compromise formation between his own tendencies and his *reflexive acceptance of the role which the patient is forcing on him*" (p. 46).

In his paper on projective identification, Sandler (1989) also suggests that the analyst's shift from a complementary identification (with the fantasied object representation) to a concordant identification (with the self-representation) in the countertransference corresponds to two distinct steps in a patient's intrapsychic employment of projective identification:

> Countertransference response due to second-stage projective identification is always based on identification with a fantasy object, and that when it appears to be identification with aspects of the self-representation, a further intrapsychic step has occurred in the patient's fantasying process; that is, a *further projective identification* has taken place into a new fantasy analyst-object which then contains projected aspects of the self [p. 23].

If I read Sandler correctly, he is suggesting that, in a concordant identification, the analyst, in his countertransference, is identifying with those parts of the self-representation which the patient has projected into the fantasy object. If this is correct, such identifications would have to be distinguished from the analyst's temporary identifications with a patient's self-representations which are not projected into object representations. It is obvious that such empathic identifications form a constant element in our daily clinical work.

In concluding his survey on projective identification, Sandler expresses a concern which, I think, is still as valid today as it was then, especially his second point:

> First, because projective identification is more a descriptive than an explanatory concept, and because its range of meaning is wide, its use without further elaboration provides a ready pseudoexplanation. Such pseudoexplanations are tempting, and we should be on our guard against them. If projective identification is used as an explanation, its specific meaning in the relevant context should, I think, always be given. Second, because of the close link between the concept of projective identification and our extended understanding of countertransference, it is tempting to see all feelings, fantasies, and reactions of the analyst to his patient as being an outcome of what the patient has "put into" the analyst by means of projective identification. Unfortunately, the differentiation of what belongs to the patient and what to the analyst is likely to remain with us for some time as a difficult technical problem [p. 26].

And, we might add, it is not only a technical problem but, more fundamentally, also involves differences in theoretical conceptualization.

In his paper "On Internal Object Relationships," Sandler (1990b) elaborates further on his notions of role responsiveness and actualization. He points out that the patient's aim in actualizing a particular internal fantasy relationship in reality is to achieve what Freud (1900) called an "identity of perception"; that is, "if one imagines that what one wishes for is actually achieved, then the wish will, at least temporarily, be fulfilled" (p. 867). Sandler continues,

> In order to obtain wish fulfillment the individual may seek the identity of perception in a variety of ways. The commonest of

> these is through attempting to act on the external world in order to change it so that it will conform to the unconscious wish or wishful fantasy. This is the process we can refer to as the attempt at *actualization,* the effort to make the perception of reality correspond to what is wished for [p. 868].

In the same paper, he also addresses the clinical usefulness of the concepts of "internal object" and "internal object relationship." In his view, they function

> as clinically appropriate *organizing constructs in the mind of the analyst.* All the analyst can see or know are the thoughts, fantasies, feelings, and behavior of the patient, and he can be aware of his reactions to this material. While all this may be *perceived* by the analyst, the internal objects and internal object relationships in the sense I have been describing them can only be *conceived of* as organizations *lying behind* the material brought by or elicited from the patient. Interpretations made by the analyst in terms of internal objects or internal object relations are *constructions* for the purpose of anchoring the material of the analysis within an appropriate frame of reference built up by the analyst and patient during the course of the analytic work [pp. 874–875].

Thus, in his view, the internal object "is only evident in the shape of its derivatives" (p. 875). His concluding suggestion is

> that the world of the internal objects in the nonexperiential realm be considered as *giving rise to* a fantasy and thought, to a (largely unconscious) phantom world in which we live at the same time as we live in the *real* world. This inner world is a world of unconscious ghost-object images which we have constructed during the course of development, objects in unconscious fantasy whose presence is gratifying, wish-fulfilling, and reassuring. While we can conceive of the internal objects as relatively unchanging structures, the figures in this fantasy world, derivatives of the internal objects, do change as they are updated and modified—as in the transference fantasies which are so central to our analytic work [pp. 877–878].

It is noteworthy that Sandler conceptualizes internal objects and internal object relationships as unconscious structures which can become knowable only through their derivatives. This compares to and parallels the conceptualization of repressed instinctual drive wishes which can also only be inferred from their derivatives. But as Sandler has noted elsewhere, fantasied internal object relationships do not always necessarily involve instinctual drive wishes but may primarily be motivated by the achievement of certain feeling states which have to do with security, safety, well-being, and the like.

Although Sandler (1976) in his paper on "Countertransference and Role Responsiveness" mainly focuses on interactive processes that occur in the clinical situation between the patient and the analyst, he is well aware that similar interactions occur in object relationships in everyday life. Thus the tendency to *actualize* fantasied and wished-for relationships is ubiquitous. It is based on a "complicated system of unconscious cues, both given and received. . . . This is the same sort of process that occurs not only in the aspects of transference and countertransference discussed here but in normal object relationships and in the process of temporary or permanent object choice as well" (p. 47).

Conclusion

If we think of Sandler and Joffe's (1969) paper "Toward a Basic Psychoanalytic Model," we can appreciate that, from very early on in his analytic career, it was one of Sandler's overriding aims to integrate differing psychoanalytic conceptualizations and models. Having been a member of the British Psychoanalytical Society, he was, of course, constantly confronted with the Kleinian model of object relations theory. The book *Projection, Identification, Projective Identification* (1989), which he edited, and his own chapter on projective identification in it also bear witness to these attempts at integration. Sandler (1990b) has been most explicit about these attempts in his paper "On Internal Object Relations," in which he notes that after the so-called controversial discussions of 1943

> Life in the British Society has continued . . . to be marked by controversy, but this has not been altogether a bad thing, for it has forced some members of each group to sharpen their

> arguments in order to respond more effectively to the views with which they disagreed. Inevitably, of course, a certain amount of cross-fertilization has occurred, and I hope that not too many will regard this paper as the illegitimate offspring of an unorthodox union [p. 861].

Later in the paper, Sandler speaks of the multiple models or frames of reference and emphasizes the "value of *tolerating* different theories in one's mind and trying to understand them in order to permit the theories to interact with one another, and possibly lead to clinically useful theoretical developments" (p. 862). Still later, he again highlights the advantage of struggling with the conceptualizations of others:

> I have been fortunate to have had my psychoanalytic development within a milieu in which, in order to enter into meaningful dialogue with colleagues who make use of a different theoretical framework—and with whom I have many profound disagreements—it has been necessary to put oneself in the other person's shoes in order to be able to identify areas of agreement and disagreement. I have tried to show that even though this process involves temporarily (and at times even unconsciously) identifying oneself with theoretical models that compete with one's own, the outcome can be productive [pp. 876–877].

I think Joe Sandler's work is the best proof of this.

REFERENCES

Bowlby, J. (1988), *A Secure Base.* London: Routledge.

Emde, R. N. (1988), Development terminable and interminable. *Internat. J. Psycho-Anal.,* 69:23–42.

Fonagy, P., Cooper, A. M. & Wallerstein, R. S., eds. (1999), *Psychoanalysis on the Move: The Work of Joseph Sandler.* London: Routledge.

_______ & Target, M. (2000), Mentalisation and the changing aims of child psychoanalysis. In: *Psychoanalysis in Childhood and Adolescence,* ed. K. von Klitzing, P. Tyson & D. Bürgin. Basel, Switzerland: Karger, pp. 129–139.

Freud, S. (1900), The interpretation of dreams. *Standard Edition,* 4 & 5. London: Hogarth Press, 1953.

Gampel, Y. (1999), Between the background of safety and the background of the uncanny in the context of social violence. In: *Psychoanalysis on the Move: The Work of Joseph Sandler,* ed. P. Fonagy, A. M. Cooper & R. S. Wallerstein. London: Routledge, pp. 59–74.

Jacobson, E. (1954), The self and the object world: Vicissitudes of their infantile cathexes and the influence on ideational and affective development. *The Psychoanalytic Study of the Child,* 9:75–127. New York: International Universities Press.

Kernberg, O. (1982), Self, ego, affects and instinctual drives. *J. Amer. Psychoanal. Assn.,* 30:893–917.

Sandler, J. (1960a), The background of safety. *Internat. J. Psycho-Anal.,* 41:352–356.

_______ (1960b), On the concept of superego. *The Psychoanalytic Study of the Child,* 15:128–162. New York: International Universities Press.

_______ (1962), Psychology and psychoanalysis. *Brit. J. Med. Psychol.,* 35:91–100.

_______ (1976), Countertransference and role responsiveness. *Internat. Rev. Psycho-Anal.,* 3:43–47.

_______ (1987), *From Safety to Superego.* London: Karnac Books.

_______, ed. (1989), *Projection, Identification, Projective Identification.* London: Karnac Books.

_______ (1990a), On the structure of internal objects and internal object relationships. *Psychoanal. Inq.,* 10:163–181.

_______ (1990b), On internal object relations. *J. Amer. Psychoanal. Assn.,* 38:859–880.

_______ Dare, C., Holder, A. & Dreher, A. U. (1992), *The Patient and the Analyst: The Basis of the Psychoanalytic Process.* London: Karnac Books.

_______ Holder, A., Dare, C. & Dreher, A. U. (1997), *Freud's Models of the Mind: An Introduction.* London: Karnac Books.

_______ _______ & Meers, D. (1963), The ego ideal and the ideal self. *The Psychoanalytic Study of the Child,* 18:139–158. New York: International Universities Press.

_______ & Joffe, W. (1969), Toward a basic psychoanalytic model. In: *From Safety to Superego,* ed. J. Sandler. New York: Guilford Press, 1987, pp. 235–254.

_______ & Nagera, H. (1963), Aspects of the metapsychology of fantasy. *The Psychoanalytic Study of the Child,* 18:159–194. New York: International Universities Press.

_______ & Rosenblatt, B. (1962), The concept of the representational world. *The Psychoanalytic Study of the Child,* 17:128–145. New York: International Universities Press.

_______ & Sandler, A.-M. (1978), On the development of object relations and affects. *Internat. J. Psycho-Anal.,* 59:285–296.

Schafer, R. (1999), Some reflections on the concept of enactment. In: *Psychoanalysis on the Move: The Work of Joseph Sandler,* ed. P. Fonagy, A. M. Cooper & R. S. Wallerstein. London: Routledge.

Sorce, J. & Emde, R. N. (1981), Mother's presence is not enough: Effect of emotional availability on infant exploration. *Dev. Psychol.,* 17:737–745.

Stern, D. (1985), *The Interpersonal World of the Infant.* New York: Basic Books.

Körnerstrasse 17
Hamburg 22301
Germany
alex.holder@dialeasy.de

The Influence of Joseph Sandler's Work on Contemporary Psychoanalysis

OTTO F. KERNBERG, M.D.

This overview stresses Joseph Sandler's integration of classical ego psychology with contemporary object relations theory. As part of this integration, Sandler clarified the origins and internal structure of the superego as a consequence and development of the representational world. The representational world, in turn, derives from the internalization of significant self- and object representations in the context of affect activation as fundamental motivational factors. Sandler described the transformation of internalized object relations into an unconscious template, expressed in repetitive behavior patterns, and the reactivation of its constituent object relations in the transference. In differentiating the present and past unconscious in the transference, Sandler described the role responsiveness of the analyst in the psychoanalytic situation as a specific countertransference reaction that facilitates the analysis of the object relationships activated in the transference. Sandler also explored the relationship between affects and drives and the neuropsychological capacities represented by affective and cognitive developments that jointly determine the structural characteristics of the mental apparatus.

Otto F. Kernberg, M.D. is Director, Personality Disorders Institute, New York Presbyterian Hospital–Weill Medical College of Cornell University, Westchester Division; Professor of Psychiatry, Joan and Sanford I. Weill Medical College of Cornell University; Training and Supervising Analyst, Columbia University Center for Psychoanalytic Training and Research.

I BELIEVE IT IS FAIR TO SAY THAT JOSEPH SANDLER HAS CONTRIBUTED more than anybody else to the integration of classical ego psychology with contemporary object relations theory, at both the theoretical and the clinical level. The past 30 years have witnessed the ascendance of object relations theory as an overall integrating frame of reference that links psychoanalytic metapsychology with the vicissitudes of the psychoanalytic process and facilitates the formulation of unconscious intrapsychic conflict in clinically more helpful ways than the traditional frame of reference exclusively based on the conflict between drives and defensive operations. It is a shift in perspective that has emerged simultaneously within the British psychoanalytic approaches of Melanie Klein and Ronald Fairbairn, and the Interpersonal or Cultural psychoanalytic approach derived from Harry Stack Sullivan. Within the ego-psychological approach, under the influence of Erik Erickson, Edith Jacobson, and Margaret Mahler in the United States, developments occurred to parallel what in Great Britain evolved as the contemporary ego-psychological approach of Joseph and Anne-Marie Sandler, gradually integrating, in theory and practice, an object relations model with ego-psychological formulations.

Joseph's Sandler's approach is one of careful and systematic elaboration of what might be called the "building blocks" of a contemporary ego-psychological object relations theory, carefully exploring each area of the tripartite structure on its own merits before gradually linking it into an overall theoretical frame. Joseph Sandler's early analysis of superego structures as part of the Hampstead Clinic's developmental project, and his contributions to the clarification of the origin and functions of real and ideal representations of self and objects in the ego, constituted the first steps in this integrative process. The concept of the "representational world" described both ego and superego as structures that integrated real and ideal representations of self and object, with the specific function of idealized and critical and punitive object representations as key superego components, thus linking Sandler's (1987) analysis of the superego structure with Edith Jacobson's corresponding analysis of the layers of the superego. The id or dynamic unconscious would be made up of repressed or dissociated, intolerably desired and feared primitive object relations and their corresponding extreme and overwhelming libidinal and aggressive affects.

Joseph Sandler focused on the central nature of affect activation in the psychoanalytic relationship as the starting point of his formulation that internalized object relations include not only the representations of self and object in any particular real or fantasized, desired or feared relationship, but also, and crucially, the affect linking those self- and object representations. Affectively invested and affect-driven internalized object relations are actualized in the transference not only in specific, fantasized desires and fears emerging in free associations, but also, and significantly so, in the patient's character traits, particularly the pathological character traits that emerge as transference resistances, often in the early stages of the analysis.

In the course of the elaboration of the concept and functions of internalized object relations, Joseph and Anne-Marie Sandler stressed the central importance of affects as the link between self- and object representation in any particular fantasized interaction between them. They highlighted the patient's search for safety in an optimal object relationship, that would replicate the original experiences of safety and confirm expected role relationships in the infant–mother interaction. The Sandlers pointed to the role of anxiety as signaling the dissonance between the unconsciously expected and the actually experienced relation between the self and the object. In reexamining the psychoanalytic theory of motivation, Joseph Sandler stressed the importance of affects as motivational factors, in addition to that of impulses and drive derivatives. What is actualized in the psychoanalytic process, he stressed, are affectively invested, feared, and desired object relations reflecting the unconscious conflicts embedded in the patient's internal world of object relations.

Joseph Sandler then went on to describe the intrapsychic transformations in unconscious fantasy that lead from the earliest experience in the mother–infant relationship to an internal world of desired and feared object relations that is gradually elaborated and transformed into an unconscious "template." The concept of an unconscious template became quite central in the contributions of Joseph and Anne-Marie Sandler. They described the continuities and discontinuities between the most primitive realization of unconscious fantasy in hallucinatory wish fulfillment and delusion formation, on the one hand, and the complex layers of unconscious and conscious daydreaming, and unconscious and conscious illusory transformation of the perception of present reality, on the other. They carefully differentiated this experiential conscious and unconscious world from the unconscious, nonexperiential cognitive and perceptive substructures that facilitate these object relational developments. Joseph Sandler clarified, within a contemporary ego-psychological theoretical frame, the difference between the ego as an "impersonal" set of substructures, and the "representational world" constituted by self- and object representations, ideal self- and ideal object representations, linked in wishful, affectively invested relations that reflect the gradual elaboration of drives within the internal world of object relations. Internalized object relations thus consolidate into an unconscious template, expressed in repetitive behavior patterns that, in the course of psychoanalytic exploration, may be retranslated into fantasized object relations actualized in the transference and countertransference.

The concept of an unconscious template then evolved into Sandler's formulations regarding the "present and the past unconscious." Joseph and Anne-Marie Sandler (1984) stressed the difference between actual past experiences, their internalization and elaboration in unconscious fantasy, their transformation into a template that consolidates the organization of an internal world of object relations, and the actualization of this internal world in the transference–countertransference relationship. In the process, they clarified the differences between the introjection of objects as internal structures, on the one hand, and identification as the modification of the self-representation by internalizing aspects of the object representation into it, on the other. They described the child's ongoing reshaping of the concept of the self in parallel to his gradually sorting out reality from fantasy in his perceptions of mother and significant others. And they differentiated "construction"—that is, the interpretation of an unconscious object relation actualized in the "here and now" of the transference, from the "reconstruction" of past unconscious experiences, derived from the gradual dissolution of the unconscious template into its constituent internalized object relations.

The next development of Joseph Sandler's (1976) theoretical formulations included the concept of "role responsiveness." Starting from the basic assumption that unconscious fantasy includes not simply derivatives of libidinal and aggressive drives, but specific wishes for gratifying relationships between the self and significant objects, in the context of the interactions within which such drive derivatives could be gratified, Sandler stated that unconscious fantasy takes the form of wishes for specific relationships of the self with an object represented by fantasized, desirable relations between self-representations and object representations. The individual unconsciously attempts to fulfill these wishes by bringing about relationships in reality, with real objects in the "here and now," that reflect the desired "identity of perception" with the fantasized object relationship between self and internal object. The expression of impulse derivatives is transformed into a desired interaction with an object, and the wishful fantasy includes the reaction of the object to the wishful action of the individual. Unconsciously, the individual sends out signals and behaves to induce complementary actions on the part of significant objects, and is unconsciously attuned to the role responsiveness of such objects.

These developments are particularly clear in the psychoanalytic situation, where transference developments reflect not only fantasized relations with the analyst, but unconscious efforts to induce in him or her complementary roles that correspond to the unconscious object relationships that, if realized, would fulfill unconscious wishes. The analyst's countertransference, codetermined by the patient's transference developments and by the unconscious role responsiveness of the analyst, facilitates the actualization of unconsciously fantasized object relations in the transference. If the analyst is able to tolerate the activation of such a role responsiveness, and yet contain it and utilize it for the understanding of the unconscious wish fulfillment implied in the transference, he may thus obtain a powerful tool for the interpretation of unconscious fantasy in the "here and now." Pathological character traits that emerge as transference resistances constitute the automated manifestations of unconscious object relations, and are activated to express the unconscious desire to bring about a particular interaction with the analyst, to induce a certain role responsiveness in him.

From this viewpoint, character defenses, as well as the impulses against which they are directed or that they are indirectly expressing, are actualizations of defensively activated object relations geared to avoid opposing, threatening, fantasized object relations. Role responsiveness, in short, emerges as an important aspect of the countertransference and facilitates the actualization of an unconscious conflict in the transference. Sandler's concept of role responsiveness thus emerges as a crucial complement to projective identification as described within Kleinian theory, condensing the analyst's affects and behavior unconsciously induced by the patient and the analyst's specific unconscious dispositions to resonate with that particular interaction. "Actualization," Sandler clarified, has to be differentiated from "acting out"; the latter is a defensive expression in behavior of affectively invested object relations that cannot be tolerated as the affectively invested representations of self and object in a particular fantasized desired or feared relationship.

On the basis of all these considerations, Sandler considered developmental profiles to be hierarchical organizations and not linear developments, a subtle but crucial modification of the concepts of developmental lines that emerged from the Hampstead Clinic's project. From his discussions with Anna Freud emerged an important theoretical shift, part of an inspiring and brilliant dialogue that signals the basic changes in analytic formulations of recent years.

Joseph Sandler's stress on the interactional nature of the desired, wishful object relations, and the influence of unconscious desire on the actual behavior of the significant other, reflected in a major emphasis on countertransference analysis, signifies a shift of the "one-person" psychology into a "two-person" psychology or, rather, a "three-person" psychology. This latter psychology reflects the stress, on the part of Joseph and Anne-Marie Sandler, that the analyst must tolerate the activation of his role responsiveness in the countertransference, be aware of the risk of partial actualizations of it, and contain and use it as an "outside observer" to analyze the total object relationship activated in the transference. A French psychoanalyst might say that rather than an acting and an "outside observer" the analyst symbolically becomes the "third excluded other" of early and later oedipal relationships.

The highlighting of affects as a central feature of the object relations activated in the transference, and Joseph and Anne-Marie Sandler's (1998) convincing theoretical and clinical illustrations of the motivational functions of affects, raises the question: to what extent might a further theoretical step be in place, namely, the consideration of affects as the concrete derivatives of drives that are embedded in internal object relations, and in that context, carry out the motivational functions of drives. One could ask to what extent the concept of affects proposed by Joseph Sandler, namely, affects as central subjective experiences (in contrast to the earlier psychoanalytic theory of affects as discharge products of the drives) may imply that drives always manifest themselves as libidinal or aggressive affects, and that their motivational force becomes always affective motivation. Anxiety, in this regard, would constitute the direct affective expression of the alertness to the danger threatening libidinal relations, or of aggressive impulses projected onto a source of imaginary or real danger. The affect of safety, which represents a sublimatory aspect of libidinal relations (in contrast to sexual excitement as the most direct affective expression of libido), may be contrasted to the manifold expressions of unconscious and conscious hatred and envy as dominant affects that express the aggressive drive. From this viewpoint, the drive-derived motivational forces would always be expressed by the motivational implications of wish-fulfilling fantasies of affectively invested, desired, and threatening internal object relations, a proposal that, I believe, is in consonance with Joseph and Anne-Marie Sandler's formulations.

Joseph Sandler was extremely interested not only in the contemporary theory of affect—and how it interdigitates with psychoanalytic drive theory—but also in the conceptual implications of the developmental aspects of cognitive functions. Insofar as both affects and representations of self and object depend on underlying neuropsychological capacities represented by affective and cognitive development, Sandler considered these issues of central importance in contemporary psychoanalytic studies, particularly the efforts to relate intrapsychic structures with their neuropsychological predispositions.

Regarding the application of all of these theoretical conceptions to psychoanalytic technique, Joseph and Anne-Marie Sandler, in their focus on the actualization of unconscious fantasy (reflecting wished-for and feared internal object relationships), have increased the subtlety and scope of psychoanalytic interventions, while opening up the field of derived psychoanalytic modalities of treatment, particularly psychoanalytic psychotherapy. In his private communications in recent times, Joseph Sandler stressed the importance of systematic studies of psychoanalytic psychotherapy and the related broad spectrum of psychoanalytic techniques. His untimely death has left important unfinished tasks for the psychoanalytic scientific and professional community to carry out. His visionary contributions resonate from his work in the rapprochement of British and American ego-psychological and object relations schools (Sandler et al., 1992), and in the general recognition that systematic research on psychoanalytic theory, technique, and applications is an urgent and essential task for the psychoanalytic community at large. Joseph Sandler initiated the yearly International Psychoanalytic Association Research Conferences in London and, together with Robert Wallerstein and Peter Fonagy, gradually brought about the new consciousness of the importance of psychoanalytic research that ultimately represents one of his major conceptual and institutional achievements.

Some Future Trends

Joseph Sandler's concern with conceptual clarity and his openness to developments by other disciplines are important aspects of his theoretical formulations regarding the representational world. The shift from general psychological theory concerns to the particular aspects of development is a related consequence of Sandler's thinking. Instead of an interest in a general metapsychology, there is now a developing concern with particular observations as part of empirical research, and the integration of multiple observations and methods to clarify developmental processes. Development itself is understood as probabilistic, derived from multiple experiences and environmental factors; in parallel, the study of the psychoanalytic process itself has begun to focus on particular aspects of the therapeutic interactions (R. Emde, personal communication).

Regarding Sandler's interest in the neurosciences, there is a growing awareness of "wired in" unconscious functions, reflecting both the setup of unconscious templates and underlying substructures derived from language and cognitive development as well as from early affective maturation. The neurobiological findings regarding the differences between procedural learning and declarative learning are related to the unconscious aspects of intersubjectivity; such neurobiological correlates are of definite interest in the study of the relationship between these substructures and unconscious fantasy.

Regarding psychoanalytic technique, in a paper on "Convergencies and Divergencies in Psychoanalytic Technique" (1993), I pointed to the major convergencies between Kleinian, Independent, ego psychology, and even French mainstream approaches, with the

Lacanian position remaining outside that mainstream on psychoanalytic technique. This emerging swing of the pendulum toward the integration of different approaches owes its strength mainly to Joseph Sandler, who integrated ego psychology and object relations theory by pointing to internalized object relations as the structural underpinnings of ego, superego, and id, and by stressing the clinical relevance of object relations theory to the analysis of transference and countertransference. The shift into object relations models facilitates the reintegration of Sullivanian psychology, while neuropsychology links drives with affects, so that affects and internalized object relations may be considered the building blocks of the tripartite structure.

Sandler's contributions to the concepts of enactment and actualization permit new refinement in technique leading to better understanding of patients. Sandler described how patients make their fantasy actual or alive by making the analyst assume the roles they require. Unconsciously, the patient seeks to evoke a corresponding emotional reaction in the analyst that guides him. It is possible that there is always such a reaction evoked in the analyst before he becomes able to interpret. Its importance results from the atmosphere created by the patient, rather than from what the patient says. A new reality is created in the psychoanalytic situation, and the change induced in the analyst then may permit him to understand better the relationship enacted in the transference.

The concept of actualization has brought about a shift in the emphasis from acting out to "acting in"—that is, actualization. The study of the patient's behavior in the session reveals his immediate relationship with the analyst and how it relates to the patient's relationship with his internal objects. In this way, the past unfolds itself, which makes analytic work less dependent on the history as it was told.

Regarding Joseph Sandler's concept of the present unconscious and the past unconscious, the latter is typically expressed as action scenarios, in contrast to the representational dominance in the expression of the present unconscious (Widlocher, 1999). The most important issue is that language is not simply a means of narration, but also a system of action, and both are constituents of psychic reality, a wish to bring about desired relations with a significant object, or to avoid a feared relation with it. Sandler's differentiation between the present and past unconscious permits us to pay more attention to the present unconscious and, at the same time, be aware of the manifestations of the past unconscious in action scenarios that complicate the manifestations of the present unconscious.

Another important implication of Joseph Sandler's work on the present unconscious is in the manifestations of the dynamic unconscious, not only in verbal representation and the related unconscious object relations in the transference, but in the parallel expression of unconscious fantasy, particularly of primitive unconscious conflicts that have not reached symbolic representation in the function of language but present themselves in action. Here the issue is the communication of primitive, unconscious affect that cannot be tolerated as part of preconscious functions in daydreams and verbal communication, but directly influences language, and the patient's unconscious relation to his own verbal communications as well as the direct communication of intolerable affect in the impact of the patient's linguistic style on the analyst's countertransference. Psychic reality, as Widlocher (1999) has stressed, operates simultaneously at various levels, including the plane of transference–countertransference interactions, mostly influenced by verbal communication and interaction between patient and analyst, and by means of the unconscious function of language as action that may be addressed directly to the analyst's unconscious. By the same token, the analyst's communications may address directly the patient's preconscious and his unconscious as well.

Finally, the concern over the lack of research and innovation in psychoanalytic education is a major unfinished task that Joseph Sandler has left for us, together with the other, major task that overshadows the rest, namely, that of strengthening psychoanalytic research so as to ensure the future of our science as well as of our profession.

REFERENCES

Kernberg, O. (1993), Convergences and divergences in contemporary psychoanalytic technique. *Internat. J. Psycho-Anal.,* 74:659–673.

_______ (2001), Recent developments in the technical approaches of English-language psychoanalytic schools. *Psychoanal. Quart.,* 70:519–547.

Sandler, J. (1976), Countertransference and role responsiveness. *Internat. Rev. Psycho-Anal.,* 3:43–47.

_______ (1987), *From Safety to Superego: Selected Papers of Joseph Sandler.* New York: Guilford Press.

_______ Dare, C., Holder, A. & Dreher, A. U. (1992), *The Patient and the Analyst: The Basis of the Psychoanalytic Process.* Madison, CT: International Universities Press.

_______ & Sandler, A.-M. (1984), The past unconscious, the present unconscious, and interpretation of the transference. *Psychoanal. Inq.,* 4:367–399.

_______ & _______ (1998), *Internal Objects Revisited.* London: Karnac Books.

Widlocher, E. (1999), Presented at symposium "Psychoanalysis on the Move: A Day in Memory of Joseph Sandler," March, London.

New York University Cornell Medical Center
21 Bloomingdale Road
White Plains, NY 10605
okernberg@med.cornell.edu

Joseph Sandler's Contributions to The Concept of Countertransference

GLEN O. GABBARD, M.D.

A few months before Joe Sandler's death, he participated in an American Psychoanalytic Association panel that focused on the Controversial Discussions that occurred in the British Psychoanalytic Society from 1941 to 1945. Our plan was to revisit the controversies in the context of British psychoanalysis some 50 years later. As we designed the panel, I suggested that we have one Kleinian panelist, one contemporary Freudian panelist, and a third panelist representing the Independents.

SANDLER REFLECTED ON MY PROPOSAL FOR THE COMPOSITION OF THE panel and responded that it might be difficult to find prominent representatives of those three groups who disagreed with one another. He quipped that we were likely to find more disagreement among members of the same group than we would from analysts across groups. He went on to say that a good deal of cross-fertilization had occurred in the past half-century. Sandler observed that listening for some time to papers from the three British Society groups and living next door to Betty Joseph for many years had undoubtedly influenced his current views of theory and practice.

Glen O. Gabbard, M.D. is Brown Foundation Chair of Psychoanalysis and Professor of Psychiatry, Baylor College of Medicine; Director of Psychotherapy Education and Director of Baylor Psychiatry Clinic; Training and Supervising Analyst, Houston–Galveston Psychoanalytic Institute.

That influence takes many forms when one examines the monumental work of this towering figure in psychoanalysis. However, I focus here on the development of Sandler's view of countertransference and how it evolved in the context of his own culture—that is, the three groups of the British Psychoanalytic Society. Sandler was a bridge builder who brought disparate ideas together through creative synthetic work. Not only did he build bridges between the contemporary Freudians and the other groups of the British Society, but he also was instrumental in bringing about a rapprochement between American ego psychology, Kleinian thought, and the British School of object relations theory. Finally, in an era of wide agreement that psychoanalysis is both a one-person and a two-person psychology, Sandler was a pivotal figure in integrating those two perspectives.

Early Views of Countertransference

Of course, the narrow Freudian view of countertransference is that it interferes with analytic work. In essence, Freud regarded it as the analyst's transference to the patient. The construct was not viewed as positive or useful until the arrival of Paula Heimann's (1950) classic paper in which she made clear for the first time that the analyst's reaction might actually be a useful clue to what was happening inside the patient.

Melanie Klein did not regard Heimann's broadening of the concept of countertransference as particularly auspicious (Spillius, 1992). She worried that Heimann's perspective might allow analysts to blame their patients for countertransference problems. In her view, if the analyst was sufficiently influenced by the patient's behavior to create a countertransference response, this reaction was best understood in the narrow Freudian sense and clearly implied that the analyst required further analysis to understand the response. While it is true that in Klein's (1946, 1955) initial papers on projective identification she referred to projective contents as going *into* rather than *onto* the targeted object, she did not emphasize that this preposition implied a change in the external object as an integral part of projective identification (Spillius, 1992).

The notion that there might be an interpersonal dimension of projective identification was made explicit by a small group of British analysts in the 1950s who were influenced by Klein but extended her work further. Along with Rosenfeld (1952) and Money-Kyrle (1956), Bion (1955, 1957, 1958, 1959, 1962a, b, 1970) led the way to a more contemporary view of projective identification as involving an alteration in the targeted object. Drawing from the container–contained model, Bion emphasized that in the analytic dyad, the analyst actually feels coerced by the patient into playing a role projected by the patient as part of the patient's fantasy.

Contemporary Kleinian analysts accept the notion that the analyst's feelings may reflect the patient's attempts to evoke feelings in the analyst that they cannot tolerate themselves. Joseph (1989) noted that patients often "nudge" the analyst to behave in a manner that directly corresponds to what the patient is projecting. She even suggests that optimally the analyst must allow herself to respond to those pressures from the patient in an attenuated way because it enables the analyst to become consciously aware of the projected contents and interpret what is happening to the patient. Spillius (1992) shares the view that the analyst is always influenced to some degree by what the patient is projecting.

This trend was further reinforced by developments on the other side of the Atlantic, from both North and South America. Racker (1968) suggested that the analyst's reactions can be divided into complementary and concordant countertransferences. The former involve the analyst's identification with the projectively disavowed internal object of the patient. Racker regarded this type of identification as an instance in which the analyst's own conflicts were activated by the patient's projections. In concordant countertransferences, the analyst identifies with a self-representation within the patient—an empathic link between patient and analyst.

Grinberg (1979) further distinguished countertransference by coining the term *projective counteridentification*. In this variation, the analyst introjects an affective state associated with the patient's object representation that comes almost entirely from the patient. He contrasted this with Racker's complementary countertransference reaction, which was regarded as a function of the patient's projection, corresponding with certain aspects of the analyst's own unconscious conflicts.

Meanwhile, in North America, Ogden (1979, 1982) elaborated on Bion's view of projective identification by postulating three steps inherent in the process: (1) an aspect of the self is projectively disavowed by unconsciously placing it in someone else; (2) the projector exerts interpersonal pressure that coerces the other person to experience or unconsciously identify with that which has been projected; and (3) the recipient of the projection (in the analytic situation) processes and contains the projection, leading to reintrojection by the patient in a modified form. Ogden (1992) subsequently emphasized that these three steps should not be construed literally as a linear sequence. These related aspects of projective identification create a dialectic in which the patient and analyst enter into a relationship in which they are simultaneously separate but also "at one" with each other. This dialectic of inner penetration of two subjectivities creates a unique third subjectivity.

Role Responsiveness

When Sandler (1976) published his seminal paper on role responsiveness, he was in the midst of reconsidering the psychoanalytic psychology of object relationships. He felt that the classic view of transference as a displacement of the patient's libidinal or aggressive energic cathexis from a past object to the person of the analyst was an inadequate and archaic explanation of what happens in the analytic setting. Sandler viewed the expression of unconscious wishes as occurring in the context of fantasies involving the self and an object in an interaction where each is assigned a particular role. He felt that transference attempted to *actualize* these role relationships and the relationship between the analyst and patient. In this model, the patient would prod the analyst into behaving in ways that conformed to the internal role relationship. In the course of an analysis, then, a series of role relationships would emerge in which the patient cast herself in one role while casting the analyst in a complementary role.

In keeping with this conceptual model of the analytic encounter, Sandler (1976) emphasized that free-floating attention is only a partial account of the analyst's frame of mind. He suggested that *free-floating responsiveness* was of equal importance. Part of the useful countertransference, in Sandler's view, was the analyst's overt attitudes, behaviors, and reactions as he responded naturally to the "prodding" of the patient. In this sense, he departed from the narrow

Freudian construction of countertransference as a phenomenon that reflected *only* the analyst's past and unresolved difficulties:

> However, I want to suggest that very often the irrational response of the analyst, which his professional conscience leads him to see entirely as a blind spot of his own, may sometimes be usefully regarded as a compromise formation between his own tendencies and *his reflexive acceptance of the role which the patient is forcing on him* [Sandler, 1976, p. 46].

Concerned that he might be misconstrued as going further than he intended, Sandler (1976) also stated that he was categorically opposed to the idea that all feelings in the analyst can be attributed to what the patient has induced or imposed on the analyst. To distance himself a bit from his Kleinian colleagues, he also argued that the complicated system of unconscious cues involved in these interactions were not adequately explained by *projective identification* or the notion of putting parts of oneself into the analyst. On the other hand, anticipating much of our contemporary view of countertransference, he noted that certain aspects of the analyst role-responsive countertransference might need to be carried into action before the analyst was aware of the role in which he had been cast.

Character and Countertransference

Five years after his paper on role responsiveness, Sandler (1981) made a highly creative contribution to the psychoanalytic understanding of character. Up to this point, character was primarily regarded as a defensive mastery of childhood instinctual conflict, largely influenced by the contributions of Wilhelm Reich (1933). In a continued expansion of his theory of internal object relationships, Sandler suggested that limiting the view of character to instinctual conflicts and a repertoire of defense mechanisms failed to take into account the interactional aspects of character. Using countertransference as a starting point, Sandler regarded at least some personality traits as "evocative" in the sense that they are designed to actualize responses in others that reflect an unconscious fantasy involving a wished-for role relationship. He referred to this constellation of traits as "character transferences." Some individuals, for example, may behave in an ingratiating way that leaves others feeling manipulated. Another type of character transference involves sadistic behavior designed to elicit masochistic responses in others or vice versa.

Sandler reasoned that a child naturally learns how to initiate wish-fulfilling responses from others and that these developmental strategies are carried into adulthood. In other words, object-related character traits involve ways of evoking responses from others that fulfill a longed-for mode of relatedness. In keeping with his longstanding theory of motivation, he suggested that the wish-fulfilling aspect went beyond instinctual gratification by also including wished-for safety and affirmation. Sandler also anticipated the contemporary concern about the mechanism by which traumatic childhood relationships are repeated, despite their negative aspects. He emphasized that even distressing and unpleasant relationships may provide affirmation, reassurance, and safety in that they recreate the predictable and familiar environment of childhood.

Sandler's notion that character traits involve unconscious techniques for imposing on another person a way of experiencing and behaving has important diagnostic implications. In an era when personality disorders are often diagnosed by checklists in response to direct questions, Sandler's model of character stresses the importance of the clinician's reactions to what the patient does in a diagnostic interview. In other words, part of a patient's character is the "dance" that he or she creates with an interviewer that reveals a wished-for internal object relationship as it becomes externalized in the interpersonal situation (Gabbard, 1997). The role in which the interviewer is placed may be critical to understanding the nature of the patient's difficulties in object relations outside the clinical setting. Sandler always stressed, however, that the clinician's response to the enticement to join in the "dance" may vary from one person to the next. Some clinicians may enact the role that the patient is actualizing. Others may note the attempt to actualize and slough it off. Still others may unconsciously reject the role in which they have been cast.

Although I emphasize the bridging function of Sandler's writings in the context of the different groups within the British Society, I think it is also fair to recognize that Sandler acknowledged a debt to Anna Freud's thinking in developing his conceptualization. He once observed, for example, that Anna Freud had introduced a "whole class of what might be called object-related defenses, which involved reversal of roles or some combination of identification and projection" (Sandler, 1983, p. 41). Hence, in his view, there was only a small step between object-related defenses and character transferences.

Countertransference and Projective Identification

Throughout his writing, Sandler was careful to point out the potential misuse and overgeneralization of Klein's construct of projective identification. He emphasized that projective identification occurred in fantasy and that the parts of the self were put into a fantasy object (i.e., an *internal* object rather than an *external* object). Because of this deemphasis on the interactive aspects, Sandler (1987) felt that projective identification (as originally described by Klein) had little connection with countertransference: "Transference reflects infantile object relationships . . . and is *a fantasy about the analyst* which needs to be analyzed. . . . Countertransference, in its turn, is scarcely mentioned, and when it is . . . it is regarded as a hindrance to the analyst's technique" (p. 17).

Sandler was, of course, thoroughly familiar with Bion's extension of Klein's original view. He credited Bion with the elaboration of projective identification as an externalization of parts of the self—or of an internal object—directly into an external object. While he could accept the idea that projection occurs *into* an external object, he thought it was stretching the concept to the breaking point when Bion included the analyst's containment, detoxification, and return to the patient as part of the definition of projective identification. In his view, the containment of the analyst was a separate phenomenon.

One of Sandler's main concerns appears to have been that projective identification had become an all-encompassing term that had lost its specificity. He entitled his 1993 paper, based on his summary at the 38th International Psychoanalytic Congress in Amsterdam that year, "On Communication from Patient to Analyst: Not Everything Is Projective Identification." In this essay, he cautioned against the assumption that all subjective experiences that analysts feel during a session have been put into them by the patient. He worried that such a sweeping generalization would lead to "wild countertransference analysis" (Sandler, 1993, p. 1104).

He felt strongly that projective identification should be regarded as a defense and that what distinguished it was that the projected self- or object representation was thrust upon the external object. He contrasted it with primary identification, which he viewed as a fundamental and automatic mirroring process closely related to analytic empathy. He uses as an example an incident that stayed in his mind some 35 years. He had been walking along a crowded London street when a man in front of him suddenly slipped off the edge of the pavement. Sandler noted that he immediately righted himself as though he were also about to stumble into the street. A direct emotional reaction to the patient's material or behavior was not projective identification, in Sandler's view, "unless it is unconsciously intended to evoke such a reaction in the analyst" (Sandler, 1993, p. 1105).

Despite Sandler's efforts to define projective identification in a clinically useful and specific manner, a convergence between his view of role responsiveness and the British Kleinian's view of projective identification has occurred over the last decade or so. Spillius (1992) characterized his concept of actualization in the process of role responsiveness as a colloquial term for the same process described by Joseph when she said the patient unconsciously nudges the analyst into behaving in a way that is consistent with what has been projected. Similarly, in the 1999 panel on the Controversial Discussions at the American Psychoanalytic Association meeting that postdated Sandler's death, Britton opined that there is no significant difference between the contemporary usage of projective identification and Sandler's notion of role responsiveness.

Common Ground

In my 1995 paper entitled "Countertransference: The Emerging Common Ground," I stressed that countertransference has become conceptualized as a joint creation involving contributions from both analyst and analysand, a view that had taken hold among contemporary Freudians, modern Kleinians, relational theorists, and constructivists. To a large extent, Sandler paved the way for this consensus when he spoke of role responsiveness as a compromise between the analyst's psychology and what was induced in the analyst by the patient's behavior. In the ensuing years, a number of American ego psychologists followed suit in their emphasis on enactment.

McLaughlin (1991) defined enactments as involving defensive interactions between analyst and patient that were experienced by either one as a consequence of the behavior in the other. The link between Sandler's ideas and the concept of enactment is even clearer in Chused's (1991) definition: "Enactments occur when an attempt to actualize a transference fantasy elicits a countertransference reaction" (p. 629). Jacobs (1993) observed that what the analyst experiences may provide a valuable source of information about the inner experiences of the patient.

Roughton (1993) pointed out that enactment as an actualization of a countertransference response was virtually identical to role responsiveness. He also showed the similarity between that view and the most widely held American view of projective identification, the one based on Odgen's (1979) paper. Roughton speculated that perhaps the most fundamental difference in the common usage of the term was that projective identification was typically used to describe more primitive patients, whereas enactment was commonly applied to the more typical neurotically organized analytic patient.

Along with this consensus about the joint construction of the countertransference response is the view that enactments and role responsiveness are inevitable in the course of any psychoanalytic treatment. Relational analysts, such as Mitchell (1988) and Aron (1991), have reached similar conclusions. Mitchell noted that the "analyst is regarded, at least to some degree, as embedded within the analysand's relational matrix. There is no way for the analyst to avoid his assigned roles and configurations within the analysand's relational world" (p. 292).

To be sure, there are still some differences in the way that analysts of different persuasions construe the relative contributions of patient and analyst to countertransference phenomena. Projective identification generally connotes aspects of the patient that have activated certain internal representations or feelings in the analyst in a powerfully coercive way. The countertransference feeling is often experienced as "ego alien" because the repressed components that have been stimulated in the analyst are unfamiliar or disavowed. When American ego psychologists write about countertransference enactment, they generally focus more on the contributions from the analyst's unconscious conflicts and less on the coercion by the patient's projections. Hence, one can postulate a gradient with projective identification on one end, role responsiveness in the middle, and countertransference enactment on the other end with considerable overlap in between (Gabbard, 1995).

Looking back on the evolution of Sandler's ideas, one cannot avoid the sense that he brought together a great many analysts of different persuasions. With his solid common sense, his impressive synthetic mind, and his carefully reasoned style of argument, he demonstrated that both a one-person and a two-person psychology are relevant to psychoanalytic theory and practice. He also illusatrated convincingly that patients always work to transform the analyst into a transference object that is part of an unconscious wished-for role relationship within the patient. His openness to object relations thinking encouraged other contemporary Freudians and American ego psychologists to broaden their notion of motivation to include wishes that involved objects, not simply instinctual gratification.

Certainly, one of Sandler's fundamental contributions to psychoanalysis was his broadening of our understanding of unconscious fantasy. In all of his writing he made it clear that unconscious fantasy included much more than simple derivatives of aggressive and libidinal drives. Wishes for specific types of gratifying relationships between the self and others were always considered an essential part of unconscious fantasy in Sandler's view. Indeed, the drive derivatives were regarded as transformed into a desired interaction with an object.

Finally, through his ongoing efforts to understand countertransference, Joseph Sandler was a role model within the British Society for the maintenance of intellectual rigor while also allowing for peaceful coexistence of different theories and cross-fertilization from one theory to another.

REFERENCES

Aron, L. (1991), The patient's experience of the analyst's subjectivity. *Psychoanal. Dial.,* 1:29–51.

Bion, W. R. (1955), Language and the schizophrenic. In: *New Directions in Psychoanalysis,* ed. M. Klein, P. Heimann & R. E. Money-Kyrle. London: Tavistock, pp. 220–239.

_______ (1957), Differentiation of the psychotic from the nonpsychotic personalities. In: *Second Thoughts: Selected Papers on Psycho-Analysis.* New York: Aronson, 1984, pp. 43–64.

_______ (1958), On arrogance. In: *Second Thoughts: Selected Papers on Psycho-Analysis.* New York: Aronson, 1984, pp. 86–92.

_______ (1959), Attacks on linking. In: *Second Thoughts: Selected Papers on Psycho-Analysis.* New York: Aronson, 1984, pp. 93–109.

_______ (1962a), The psycho-analytic study of thinking, II: A theory of thinking. In: *Second Thoughts: Selected Papers on Psycho-Analysis.* London: Heinemann, 1967, pp. 110–119.

_______ (1962b), *Learning from Experience.* New York: Aronson, 1983.

_______ (1970), *Attention and Interpretation: A Scientific Approach to Insight in Psycho-Analysis and Groups.* New York: Aronson, 1983.

Chused, J. F. (1991), The evocative power of enactments. *J. Amer. Psychoanal. Assn.,* 39:615–639.

Gabbard, G. O. (1995), Countertransference: The emerging common ground. *Internat. J. Psycho-Anal.,* 76:475–485.

_______ (1997), Guest editorial: Finding the "person" in personality disorders. *Amer. J. Psychiat.,* 154:891–893.

Grinberg, L. (1979), Countertransference and projective identification. In: *Countertransference,* ed. L. Epstein & A. H. Feiner. New York: Aronson, pp. 375–405.

Heimann, P. (1950), On counter-transference. *Internat. J. Psycho-Anal.,* 31:81–84.

Jacobs, T. J. (1993), The inner experiences of the analyst: Their contribution to the analytic process. *Internat. J. Psycho-Anal.,* 74:7–14.

Joseph, B. (1989), *Psychic Equilibrium and Psychic Change: Selected Papers of Betty Joseph,* ed. M. Feldman & E. B. Spillius. London: Tavistock/Routledge.

Klein, M. (1946), Notes on some schizoid mechanisms. In: *Envy and Gratitude and Other Works, 1946–1963.* New York: Delacorte Press/Seymour Lawrence, pp. 1–24.

_______ (1955), On identification. In: *Envy and Gratitude and Other Works, 1946–1963.* New York: Delacorte Press/Seymour Lawrence, pp. 141–175.

McLaughlin, J. T. (1991), Clinical and theoretical aspects of enactment. *J. Amer. Psychoanal. Assn.,* 39:595–614.

Mitchell, S. A. (1988), *Relational Concepts in Psychoanalysis: An Integration.* Cambridge, MA: Harvard University Press.

Money-Kyrle, R. E. (1956), Normal counter-transference and some of its deviations. *Internat. J. Psycho-Anal.,* 37:360–365.

Ogden, T. H. (1979), On projective identification. *Internat. J. Psycho-Anal.,* 60: 357–373.

_______ (1982), *Projective Identification and Psychotherapeutic Technique.* New York: Aronson.

_______ (1992), The dialectically constitute/decentered subject of psychoanalysis, II: The contributions of Klein and Winnicott. *Internat. J. Psycho-Anal.,* 73:613–626.

Racker H. (1968), *Transference and Counter-transference*. New York: International Universities Press.

Reich, W. (1933), *Character-Analysis: Principles and Technique for Psycho-Analysts in Practice and in Training,* 2nd ed., trans. T. P. Wolfe. New York: Orgone Institute Press, 1945.

Rosenfeld, H. A. (1952), Notes on psycho-analysis of the super-ego conflict of an acute schizophrenic patient. In: *New Directions in Psycho-Analysis*. London: Tavistock, 1955, pp. 180–219.

Roughton, R. E. (1993), Useful aspects of acting out: Repetition, enactment, and actualization. *J. Amer. Psychoanal. Assn.,* 41:443–472.

Sandler, J. (1976), Countertransference and role responsiveness. *Internat. Rev. Psycho-Anal.,* 3:43–47.

_______ (1981), Character traits and object relationships. *Psychoanal. Quart.,* 50: 694–708.

_______ (1983), Reflections on some relations between psychoanalytic concepts and psychoanalytic practice. *Internat. J. Psycho-Anal.,* 64:35–46.

_______ (1987), The concept of projective identification. In: *Projection, Identification, Projective Identification,* ed. J. Sandler. Madison, CT: International Universities Press, pp. 13–26.

_______ (1993), On communication from patient to analyst: Not everything is projective identification. *Internat. J. Psycho-Anal.,* 74:1097–1107.

Spillius, E. B. (1992), Clinical experiences of projective identification. In: *Clinical Lectures on Klein and Bion,* ed. R. Anderson. London: Tavistock/Routledge, pp. 59–73.

Department of Psychiatry
Baylor College of Medicine
6655 Travis, Suite 500
Houston, TX 77030
ggabbard@bcm.tmc.edu

The Representational World and Affect

ARNOLD M. COOPER, M.D.

The concept of the representational world, first devised to accommodate the research data of the Hampstead Index and intended to supplement the structural point of view, has since expanded into a central conceptual tool of contemporary psychoanalysis. As developed by the Sandlers, affective states and experiences are the core of all mental representations, giving psychological meaning, force, and direction to the objects represented. The emphasis on affective components, conscious and unconscious, has enriched psychoanalysis by fostering communication with neighboring disciplines. A clinical vignette illustrates the embeddedness of affective valences in internal representations.

The concept of the representational world has been one of the most useful ideas in contemporary psychoanalysis and has played a major role in the development of our current psychoanalytic thinking. The concept was developed by Sandler and Rosenblatt (1987) in an effort to understand better the accumulated empirical research data of the Hampstead Index. They were searching for a frame of reference that would allow them to conceptualize, psychoanalytically, the emotional and relational world in which the child actually dwelled and developed. The idea of a representational world originally was developed to provide a "useful supplementary frame of

---

Arnold M. Cooper, M.D. is Stephen B. Tobin and Dr. Arnold M. Cooper Professor Emeritus in Consultation Liaison Psychiatry, Weill–Cornell Medical College; Training and Supervising Analyst, Columbia Psychoanalytic Center; Past President, American Psychoanalytic Association.

reference to both the topographical and the structural theories of the mind and was in no way intended to replace these theories" (p. xix). In fact, representational theory has gone a long way toward altering our uses of topographic and structural points of view, perhaps, replacing them.

While the idea was originally framed within the context of ego psychology, with care taken by Sandler and Rosenblatt to maintain traditional points of view, the ideas of a representational world have so tightly meshed with object relations theory that the roots in ego psychology are no longer so apparent. As Sandler (1987) said in his Preface to *From Safety to Superego,*

> I believe it to be vital that psychoanalytic theory be formulated in such a way that the bridges between psychoanalysis and neighboring disciplines be widened and their number increased, also that communication between psychoanalysts and workers in related fields may be facilitated and findings in other areas can in turn influence the theory of psychoanalysis [p. 58].

From the very beginnings of their advocacy of the concept of representation, the authors were aware of the complexity of what was being represented. It was never their view that the representational world was either a duplicate of what had been presented to the senses or an independently maintained, solid inner structure of what had been perceived or experienced or imagined. Affect was always an intrinsic part of the representational world. All representations are a part of the flux of feeling-states, shaping them and shaped by them. To quote Sandler (1987), "In general we can say that the ideational content of the experiential field is embedded in a matrix of feelings, and these feelings are the essential basis upon which the nature and direction of adaptive action of the mental apparatus is taken" (p. 269). While Sandler and Rosenblatt were particularly concerned to understand self and other representations as a part of their deepening insights into the superego and problems of self-esteem regulation, Sandler in his later work emphasized the now generally accepted notion that any internal representation of self or object is a sense of the self and/or the object in an interaction, with feelings as the medium of exchange that determines the "shape," to use Sandler's word, of the self and/or object at any given moment.

Beginning with his work, "The Background of Safety," it was clear that Sandler (1962) had placed feeling states at the center of his understanding of psychoanalytic psychology. In the foreword to *From Safety to Superego,* Wallerstein says,

> And in this whole evolving edifice [of Sandler's ideas] one sees gradually the transition in both concept and language from an economics and dynamics of drives and energies, of discharges and restraining structures, to an economics and dynamics of feeling states reflecting the full range from anxiety, depression, and pain to well-being and safety [p. xii].

I note in passing that Wallerstein's and Sandler's notion of the full range of positive emotion does not seem to get past safety and well-being to joy, love, ecstasy, and so on. Perhaps British restraint. The important point, however, as Sandler stressed repeatedly, is that the ego's major, perhaps sole, function is adaptation, and the most important activity it undertakes in the effort to achieve successful adaptation is the regulation of feeling states.

To illustrate, let me quote Sandler further:

> The primitive sensorium of the infant is dominated by chaotic and intense feeling experiences that become increasingly linked with other sensory contents as development proceeds. The development of perception and of the distinction between self and nonself, and between self and objects, can be seen as a consequence of the child's need to control and to regulate feelings (which are affected both by the drives and by objects in the outer world). Inasmuch as the child's objects play a vital role in this regulation, their representation becomes bound up with feeling associations of a most intense and varied sort. We could say that as a consequence, self- and object representations receive an increasing abundance of *feeling cathexes* as development proceeds. The feelings involved may be crude and primitive, but may also later be of the most refined and asensual sort (we can speak here of *value cathexes*). We should also add that, in addition to feelings derived from instinctual tension and discharge, those derived from postdischarge gratification (well-being) and feelings of safety and of "function pleasure" are also significant [p. 253].

I think it fair to say that Sandler left no doubt that in his view feelings or affect states were not only an aspect of the representational world, but were constitutive of it.

In terms of contemporary neuroscience one could suggest that the representational world is a dynamic set of interrelated brain networks that are at every moment active among the entire range of brain and mental structures, including those responsible for current perceptions, implicit and explicit memory systems, conscious affect states, and affects that are out of awareness. They are part of the implicit and procedural memories that are currently activated, including state-dependent affective and memory arousals, as well as needs and fantasies, conscious and unconscious, that are aroused by the current experience. It is likely that every mental experience, whether generated internally in fantasy, or externally through perceptual experience, activates representations and is accompanied by complex affective states that include affects that are part of similar experiences from the past and that remain a part of the representation of that newer experience in the future. It is reasonable to assume that each of these newer experiences results in some change in the brain centers underlying complex experience and that these centers are altered to some degree each time they are activated. These subtle alterations may over time shift quantity into quality. Recent work indicates that all mental activities involve large areas of brain activation, not only the modules measured in cognitive neuroscience experiments.

Sandler never conceived of representations as static, or existing as homonculi in the mind; rather, I believe that his views were always in accord with modern nonlinear dynamic systems theory. What gives structure and a degree of predictability to this complex makeup of a representation is the patterning imposed by the relative stability of adaptive aims and, particularly where neurosis is involved, by the inhibition of novel perceptions, feelings, and actions. This fixity is probably largely encoded in procedural memory.

As Joseph Sandler, and later Anne-Marie Sandler, developed the basic psychoanalytic model and subsequently the "three-box" theory of mental functioning, it was apparent that he accounted for facts of stability and predictability in mental life, perhaps particularly the mental life of neurotics, while giving full range to the degrees of freedom that allow for new behaviors and experiences. He even developed a theory of persistence to account for his observation that newly learned capacities, or the development of new mental structures, do not erase older patterns but functionally replace them in the present—ideas fully in accord with newer research findings in neuroscience and psychology.

Sidney Blatt et al. (1997) in a special issue of *Review of General Psychology* wrote, "The emphasis on mental representation in psychoanalytic object relations theory, in attachment theory and research, in developmental psychology, and in social cognition has had a major impact recently on personality assessment" (p. 357). They continued,

> Theoretical formulations and empirical investigations indicate that mental representations or cognitive-affective schemas play a central role in personality development and organization. The assessment of the content and structure of mental representations provides a basis for evaluating aspects of normal development, as well as of therapeutic change in long-term intensive treatment of seriously disturbed patients. The content and structure of mental representations can also provide a basis for differentiating among various forms of psychopathology and for constructing a more effective diagnostic taxonomy [p. 368].

The concept of mental representation, in its current usage, including cognitive and affective components, is a core of research in vast areas of psychological study, as Sandler hoped would be the case. These views of the internal world of representations preserve our psychoanalytic experience while allowing us to further the exchange of ideas with researchers in neighboring disciplines.

To illustrate this integration of affect into representational schemas, consider the following rather banal clinical vignette. Mrs. L is in the sixth year of a treatment that included periods that would fit most definitions of psychoanalysis, as well as periods of psychoanalytic psychotherapy. She is a woman of unusual intelligence, beauty, and talents in her early 50s, who was considerably successful in her vocation but never felt personally satisfied or appreciated for her achievements or the position she attained. Although she and her family were part of a large social group, she lived her personal life in a rather paranoid, self-enclosed world largely held together by her strong religious beliefs. The entire period of our work together had been characterized by constant emotional turmoil, including marital disruptions, catastrophic illness of children, financial emergencies, and vocational crises.

While each of these experiences was "genuine" in that the external circumstances were not entirely of her making, it also seemed clear that at least one purpose was achieved by this never-ending sense of commotion, confusion, and imminent danger: it was not possible for the two of us to feel that we were in the room alone, together. There were always intruding events and characters that precluded our establishing intimacy and giving focus to our relationship. I knew enough of her previous relationships to be convinced that the distance I felt from her and the danger I believed she sensed from me had many precursors and had characterized all of her relationships throughout her life. Although she knew many people and was sought after socially, she had never had a close woman friend and her romances before marriage had all ended with feelings of betrayal. She married someone who seemed reliable but unromantic, sexually unexciting, and emotionally insensitive. She was only partly right, however: he was unreliable.

Mrs. L was the older of two children by three years; her brother was the favorite of both parents. Her mother was, and still is, a vain, shallow woman who seemed quite early to have seen her daughter as either a source of social gain—through her looks and brains—or as a competitor who was to be vanquished. From a quite early age, the mother used the daughter as entree into social settings; then she shamelessly competed for her daughter's boyfriends, assuming her social position. Mrs. L's father left her mother when the patient was three; several reunions and breakups followed before they permanently separated. Her father showed no interest in maintaining any kind of relationship with his daughter.

As far back as the patient can recall, it was known to everyone in the family that her father had numerous affairs. Mrs. L had always yearned for her father's love and would respond to his seductive charms, only to be repeatedly disappointed by his unpredictable abandonments. She also recalled that her mother sharply disapproved and disrupted any of her meaningful childhood friendships, making clear to the patient that she was not to waste her time with girls who lacked social status. By the time of adolescence, Mrs. L had acquaintances but never an intimate friend. She confided in no one except religious counselors, toward whom she felt ambivalently respectful, although she sensed that they never truly understood or approved of her.

Her attitude toward me had obvious components of these precursors. She had initially entered treatment with a colleague because she was depressed and seemed unable to get enough help from religious sources. Among other things, she presented a clear major depression and was, by trial and error and with considerable difficulty, medicated by a colleague. Her initial therapist rather abruptly moved away and she was referred to me with the recommendation that I was a well-known psychoanalyst. It was rapidly apparent that in her view I was a "muck-a-muck"—someone interested in maintaining the importance of his position and devoted primarily to psychoanalytic techniques for his reasons, with no interest in her uniqueness. This was another version of her mother's—and her—view of socially significant people. She had no doubt that my aim was to mold her to my theories rather than finding out who she was.

Firmly convinced of this, she made little effort to let me know her inner life or private thoughts, rarely reporting a dream, for example. But she challenged me constantly with real-life situations that posed true dangers to her well-being. I felt I could not stand by without responding to these behaviors that seemed to me highly dangerous and potentially self-destructive. I would then get caught up in the role of decent and protective friend or parent, a role that was otherwise totally absent in her experience, while she would interpret my interventions as designed solely to protect my reputation as a good doctor and not really intended for her welfare. I was also aware that these role enactments, disruptive to analytic work in many ways, were an unavoidable part of her need to prove that I really didn't give a damn and would not help, so that if I rose to her bait it proved I was merely doing my job, and, if I didn't, it confirmed her view that I, like everyone else, didn't care about her.

Interpretations seemed never to engage her beyond an intellectual response. I found myself alternately or simultaneously frustrated and enraged while deeply concerned for her well-being, frightened by her dangerous behaviors and mood swings yet drawn to her imaginative and intellectual capacities, and appalled by her extraordinary emotional narrowness while convinced she was capable of depth. She showed a startling, perhaps motivated, inability to read complex emotional behaviors in another person—and little interest in understanding complex emotions in herself. My every feeling or desire was felt by her to be a categorical demand, and she was frightened by what she felt was her automatic initial response—defiant disobedience. She was in a constant round of masochistic provocation, righteous indignation, and self-pity.

It was not the least of my frustrations that she was always late—anywhere from 5 to 40 minutes. She almost never missed a session, but during one period of financial crisis when her presence was required at her office, she asked if she could have telephone sessions with me. She knew from previous requests for telephone sessions that I did not like them and felt personally uneasy on the telephone; this time, however, there seemed little alternative and I agreed. She phoned me on time, and these sessions were surprisingly helpful to her and comfortable for me. Within a few such sessions she returned to keeping her appointments, expressing gratitude for my surprising flexibility, but regularly arriving late.

By this time in the treatment I think one could say that Mrs. L held nascent alternate, competing representations of me, creating a new version of a very old conflict. I remained on the one hand a remote, detached figure interested only in her fulfilling my needs; on the other, there was a beginning awareness that, having survived the many tests she set out for me, there was at least the possibility that I differed from the significant figures of her childhood, representing a fantasied source of warmth and support that she had long ago cynically concluded did not exist in this universe. There were the beginnings of the uncomfortable sense of cognitive and affective dissonance aroused by sharply conflicting representations of her relationship to the same, basically maternal, object. With this initial shift in the configurations of her representational world, there was a marked change in her affective state. I began to feel an interest on her part in trying to understand me, if not herself, rather than being satisfied with a blithe conviction that there was nothing to be learned about me or about anyone else that would be of the slightest use to her. Obviously, this perception of mine was a part of a mutual feeding, if you wish, in which my warmth induced hers, which induced mine, and so on.

This affective change became quite apparent at the beginning of a session in which she was almost a half-hour late and spontaneously began to speak about her lateness—something she rarely did. If I mentioned her lateness, she felt chastised, unable to consider the possibility that we might both be curious to know what it was about. On this occasion, she said,

> I was terribly nervous about coming here. I am always nervous about coming here, but it was much worse this time. I decided to come on time and had put the time aside and then couldn't decide what to wear. I always have trouble deciding what to wear, but this time it seemed overwhelming. Everything I considered seemed inappropriate.

I questioned, "Inappropriate?" She said,

> I don't really mean "inappropriate." I mean, I decided that whatever it was I was thinking of wearing, that you wouldn't like it. I knew that you would hate what I was wearing. I know that we've talked about this before and that what I'm saying probably doesn't have much to do with you personally, but it is the way I feel about everybody. My mother always criticized everything that I put on—nothing was ever right or good enough. She felt I wasn't representing her properly. I seemed especially concerned today that you should be pleased with me, but I knew that I would put on something that would displease you. I had a dream last night. I was looking at an apartment building. It seemed quite shabby, but not bad. I then drove under a tunnel or under an overpass, and when I came out, I looked at the building again and it now seemed quite shiny, almost beautiful. I knew it was the same building, but I also knew that it couldn't be the same building and I was puzzled and confused.

Discussion of the dream and her associations prior to the dream, both in this session and in the next one, led to an increasing awareness of the escalating anxiety she felt as she began to perceive me, her children, and her new boyfriend rather differently than ever before. Her relationships, both intimate and business, had in the past been characterized by a conviction that every discussion of a plan, whether trivial or major, every arrangement for a meeting or an activity, involved one person's abject surrender with hidden fury, and the other person's insensitive triumph. All of her human contacts led to feelings of disappointment. She had either been defeated or had created an envious enemy who would eventually get even with her. Friendship, compromise, mutual desires to please were foreign concepts. These matters had been interpreted at many levels numerous times, but only now did there appear to be any acknowledgment that an alternate representation of the world might be a possibility. Among other things, the dream heralded that everything might not be as it first appeared to her. In the following session, she talked about the absence of friends throughout her life and her conviction that other people had nothing to offer her and would drain her, or that they might appreciate her talents, in which case they would want to crush her.

Over the next several days, she had a series of dreams in which figures of her past appeared. She recalled no particular action, except that these individuals were there. These figures were people who modeled the worst aspects of her mother and her past social life; they were not very bright and were social-climbing, mean-spirited, and self-involved, with no interests beyond their own clothes, and so forth. In discussing these dreams, it became clear that they demonstrated that my interpretations were wrong; there was no one in the world except people who were duplicates of her mother and her mother's world.

Shortly after this discussion, Mrs. L began to be on time for almost half of her appointments, a notable change for her. It was also the time that my vacation was approaching; for the first time, she indicated genuine interest in my plans other than where would I be in case she needed me. Haltingly, almost regretfully, she indicated that she thought we were getting someplace. In the last session before my vacation, she reported dreaming that she and a friend were going up into an attic to secure some possessions. The mood of the dream was calm, and she and her friend were enjoying the attic exploration. I will not attempt to discuss the many dimensions of this dream, but Mrs. L's first association was, "I think this is the first dream I have ever had in which I am actually with someone else—the two of us are together in the dream—and it is pleasant. Something has changed."

Like every patient, Mrs. L had problems that can be discussed at many levels, with a focus on various aspects of her psychic life. One way to understand her life is through the unrelenting commitment to maintaining a unidimensional representation of the people who came in contact with her—a representation based on the most damaging aspects of her maternal relationship. This representation was sustained through an endless series of maneuvers in which every interaction with another human being proved damaging, dangerous, or hurtful. She was, of course, totally blind to her masochistic role in either producing such effects in reality or concluding that such effects had occurred when there was little evidence of them. (I have in other papers discussed what motivates a patient to maintain an emotionally loaded representational world that guarantees injury and defeat.) Mrs. L is typical, in my experience, of a large group of patients who require a prolonged period of role responsiveness, eventually creating an affective and cognitive dissonance in internal representations, before being able to process interpretations and experience insight.

We are indebted to Joseph Sandler and his collaborators, especially Anne-Marie Sandler, for their inspirational genius in leading us into the richer, more complex, affectively constructed representational world in which psychoanalytic theory and technique are now thriving.

REFERENCES

Blatt, S. J., Auerbach, J. S. & Levy, K. N. (1997), Mental representations in personality development, psychopathology, and the therapeutic process. *Rev. Gen. Psychol.,* 1:351–374.

Sandler, J. (1960), The background of safety. *Internat. J. Psycho-Anal.,* 41:352–356.

_______ (1987), *From Safety to Superego: Selected Papers of Joseph Sandler.* New York: Guilford Press.

50 East 78th Street, Suite 1C
New York, NY 10021
amcooper@bway.net

Joseph Sandler's Clinical Gift: Narrowing the Hiatus Between Psychoanalytic Experience and Theory

MELVIN BORNSTEIN, M.D.

Joseph Sandler elegantly integrated clinical experience and psychoanalytic theory in his three-box model. He unites topographical, structural, and object relations theory with the patient's experience of the lack of safety from humiliation and shame in the psychoanalytic relationship. In the three-box model, the danger of humiliation and shame is reduced by an affect of safety that is promoted by the analyst. By adding recent ideas about a developing self, I demonstrate the clinical usefulness of the three-box model.

JOSEPH SANDLER INTEGRATED CLINICAL EXPERIENCE AND psychoanalytic theory with the representational world, the affect of safety, and the three-box model. Today, Sandler's contributions enrich the versatility and creativity of clinicians in their clinical work.

Sandler conceptualized a model of the mind from the perspective of affects, experience, and interaction while maintaining the importance of drives and structures. Although the drives and structures are not experienced, they contribute to the affects, experience, and interaction in the clinical situation. Sandler described two centers of motivation

Melvin Bornstein, M.D. is Training and Supervising Analyst, Michigan Psychoanalytic Institute.

metapsychologically—the drives and structures—and experientially the intention of maintaining a state of safety.

Sandler needed a model that was based on clinical data. Although he relied on metapsychological concepts, he understood that more than metapsychology is necessary to achieve a resonance with the clinical situation. He had to synchronize subjective and metapsychological concepts. Affects would have a central role in this model.

He achieved success by creating the three-box model. With it he was able to unite facets of metapsychology and subjectivity. He was able to conceptualize a more humane atmosphere in the analytic situation than by using metapsychology alone.

In the three-box model, the first box, the past unconscious, is oriented only to the past and represents the child within the adult. It is primitive, but it is not limited to the drives. The first box consists of unconscious fantasies with problem solving, reassuring, and defensive aspects. The wishes that arise from the first box are preemptory and directed toward seeking gratification from the perspective of the past only—that is, gratification, resolution, and the undoing of experiences from the past.

The second box, the present unconscious, is oriented to the present. It also contains unconscious fantasies with problems solving, reassuring, and defensive aspects, but rather than simply being preemptory and directed toward seeking gratification from the perspective of the past only, the unconscious fantasies in the present unconscious are influenced by the demands of the present. The past unconscious intrudes upon the present unconscious. The border between the past and present unconscious is regulated by affects of danger and pain that have been associated with repression and splitting, requiring modification of the fantasies within the past unconscious to conform with the present unconscious. The modification occurs principally through the creation of transferences.

The third box, consciousness, folds into the external world. The third box borders the second box and the external world. Actually, the border between the third box and the external world is porous. Affects of humiliation and shame are the gatekeepers of the border between the second and third boxes. Motivation in the clinical situation is based on whether it is safe to express aspects of one's past and present unconscious in the third box, which has a permeable border with the external world.

The representational world comprised of representations of interacting selves, objects, and bodily states that are influenced by affects exists in the three boxes. The representational world is a valuable conceptual tool in understanding unconscious fantasies, internalization, identification, and the composition of the superego and ego ideal. The representational world rests on structures, drives, and conflicts. The principal sources of motivation within the representational world are the drives. Yet to bridge the experience of the clinical situation with the metapsychology of the representational world, Sandler moves to the second box, the present unconscious, that borders the first box, the past unconscious, and the third box, the consciousness. Since the third box is porous to the external world, whatever passes the border between the present unconscious and consciousness is expressed in the external world. The interaction at the border between the present unconscious and consciousness is modulated by an affect of safety: that is, how safe is it to be open in one's communication with one's analyst?

In the three-box model, Sandler has enabled a clinician to move from experience to metapsychology without having to step over a large conceptual hiatus. Freud's struggle with this conceptual hiatus can be seen in his ambiguous use of the term ego to represent an experiential concept, the self, and a metapsychological concept, the ego. James Strachey, in his editorial introduction to "On Narcissism" (1957) and "Ego and Id" (1961), points out that the meaning Freud attached to *das Ich* was gradually modified. "At first," says Strachey, "he used the term without any great precision, as we might speak of 'the self.'" Strachey also points out, in his introduction to the later paper, "that it seems possible to detect two main uses: one in which the term distinguishes a person's self as a whole . . . from other people, and the other in which it denotes a particular part of the mind characterized by special attributes and functions." He adds, "In some of his intervening works, particularly in connection with narcissism, the 'ego' seems to correspond rather to the 'self.'" In a footnote, Strachey remarks that in a few places in the *Standard Edition, das Ich* has been translated by "the self."

Many writers—Peterfreund (1973), Holt (1975), Gill and Holtzman (1976), Klein (1976), Stolorow (1978), and Lichtenberg (1989)—have suggested eliminating metapsychology entirely. They argue that drives, energy, and structure are mechanistic and positivistic concepts that are too far from experience to be clinically useful. Each suggests a more experience-centered model for psychoanalysis.

Modell (1993) and Meissner (1986), who share Sandler's commitment to improving integration between experience and metapsychology, have proposed their own models. Modell stresses the importance of maintaining a one- and two-person model for psychoanalysis. He proposes the use of the self as metapsychological structure within a tripartite system and a self that is experienced as the center of motivation.

Meissner (1986) also addresses this issue of self from the perspectives of structure and experience. He argues that the conceptualization of the self in psychoanalysis may be elaborated to include the self as personal agency, the center of subjectivity, complex personal qualities, the integration of intrapsychic structures, and object relations. He recommends the use of the self as epiphenomena that integrates many facets of experience and structure.

Because of Sandler's devotion to the integration of theory and clinical experience, he explored the superego, ego ideal, and the conceptualization of the representational world (Sandler, 1987). In the clinical situation, the superego and ego ideal were not seen as whole structures; they were seen through their component parts, that is, internalized objects or precursors of the superego and ego ideal. The internalized objects that were infused with qualities of narcissism comprised part of the representational world and expressed in transferences and countertransferences.

In the clinical application of the representational world, Sandler was able to illuminate therapeutic action as involving the internalization of fragmented aspects of experience into a more coherent whole because of an increased affect of safety against humiliation and shame. Behrends and Blatt (1985) describe this process of therapeutic action as similar to the separation-individuation that leads to internalization in development. In this individuation and internalization process, experienced incompatibilities provoke a sense of limitation and dissociation of the self because of the unresponsiveness of the other person. The person is able to preserve the psychologically significant aspects of the previous gratifying involvement through internalization. The same process comprises therapeutic action in the therapeutic relationship. The similarity between the process of individuation and internalization in development and in therapeutic action has been described by Loewald (1960), Stone (1961), Stolorow (1978), and Meissner (1986).

The essential task of the clinician who follows the model is maintaining an affect of safety by keeping humiliation and embarrassment at a workable level. Sandler counseled that to go further with the model, the aim of the analyst would have to be considered. In a paper cowritten with Anne-Marie Sandler on the three-box model (1984), they describe what I believe to be a generally accepted aim of the analyst's role in an analysis:

> Because we cannot be satisfied with Freud's statement that analysis simply aims to make the unconscious conscious or to replace id by ego, we describe our ideas about the aim of analysis. It is our understanding that the analyst aims to help the patient eventually accept the infantile wishful aspect of himself that has aroused painful conflict and become threatening during the course of his development. Consequently, they strive to get the patient to tolerate the derivatives of these parts of himself in his conscious thinking and fantasies. To put it another way, a major analytic goal is to get the patient to become friends with the previously unacceptable parts of his self to get on good terms with previously threatening wishes and fantasies. To do this means that the analyst has to provide, through his interpretations and the way he gives them an atmosphere of tolerance of the infantile, the perverse, and the ridiculous an atmosphere which the patient can make part of his own attitude toward himself, which he can internalize along with the understanding he has reached in his joint work with the analyst [Sandler and Sandler, 1984].

Essentially, by communication through language, the patient is able to accept the content of the first two boxes, as the derivatives of these boxes become part of the content of the third box. With an atmosphere of safety that the analyst helps establish, the patient overcomes the barrier to the external world and is able to communicate the content of the third box to the analyst.

Rapaport (1944), in describing the methodology of psychoanalysis, wrote that the role of the analyst is to carry communication to its last consequence—taking responsibility for elimination of any and all obstacles to free association. The last consequence is the freedom to associate that enables the patient to communicate derivatives of his infantile life through the three boxes to the analyst who is part of the external world. Loewald (1960) states:

> The purpose of an analysis is to establish communication between the structures of mind. The capability to communicate the derivatives without resistances results in the patient's ability to gain a greater coherence to their self with a more open interchange with the parts of themselves and the external world.

Following Sandler's model, we can see that the humiliation and shame that are set at the border of the third box with its access to reality are based on the danger of narcissistic injury. Patients cannot reveal parts of themselves to the analyst without resistance because of the conviction that if they do, the humiliation and shame will be unbearable. The analyst through the analytic setting, attitude, and the use of interpretation—especially transference interpretation—offers safety from the anticipated overwhelming humiliation and shame.

The three-box model addresses the subjectivity of how one lives with her internal and external worlds and the metapsychology that helps in understanding the components of the internal and external world. The third box, consciousness, which borders the present unconscious and the external world, helps us focus on the paradox of being alone with one's internal world while being connected to the external world. We live with others while we live within ourselves. The three-box model helps us see that we are Janus-faced, looking inward and outward simultaneously (Modell, 1993).

The two points of view—whether humans are object seeking or drive gratifying—have been fundamental in psychoanalytic theorizing since Freud introduced his basic ideas. The debate that we are not drive gratifying but object seeking is the essential position of object relations theory (Fairbairn, 1952; Guntrip, 1971). Winnicott's (1958) description of baby and mother as the fundamental unit of human motivation is part of this tradition. Freud and the classical analysts argue that the impact of drives and conflicts between the structures of the mind serve as the basic element in psychoanalytic understanding, which is not fully addressed by the object relations theorist. Greenberg and Mitchell (1983) have concluded that the two perspectives are not reconcilable.

Because of the proliferation and depolarization of theoretical positions within psychoanalysis during the past 20 years, most psychoanalysts today are able to use facets of a number of theories and viewpoints in their work. They actually utilize both perspectives. Sandler explained that at best our theories and models are incomplete, and flexibility in the meaning and application of concepts is required for the analyst to be an effective clinician. He suggested that most psychoanalysts have a public and private perception of what they do in the clinical situation. With greater public flexibility in describing what psychoanalysts do in the clinical situation, the gap between public and private perceptions of clinical work is narrowing.

Although a subjective perspective is part of the three-box model because affect is central and the interaction of the analyst and patient in maintaining an affect of safety is significant, the self does not play a prominent role in the three-box model. For a clinician to be able to utilize the three-box model and remain close to experience in the clinical situation, a self that is experienced, that functions as an agency, and has the capacity to relate is a necessary concept. The experience of two interacting and evolving selves in the clinical situation is set between the tension of maintaining a repetition of sequestered parts of the patient and the transformation of the sequestered parts into improved capacity to communicate one's story to the analyst with more wholeness of the self and relatedness to the analyst. This experience, ongoing throughout an analysis, is enhanced by an affect of safety over humiliation and shame as the patient communicates from the past to present unconscious and to the analyst in the external world.

A patient begins his session by speaking about a dull weekend with lifeless feelings. He remarks on the contrast to feeling so alive and in touch with himself the week before. He says he feels restless and does not have anything important to discuss. He reiterates his disappointment in his wife because of her lack of involvement with him over the weekend. He is tired of always prodding to enliven her.

I have heard this refrain many times. I begin feeling distant, bored, restless, and dead. I lose track of where we are in the session. I attempt to reorient myself to his story, but I am unable to develop any idea of what is going on. I feel locked in an interaction with his complaints. I am no longer certain what I am feeling. It is as if I cannot act. I feel that he is controlling me.

I begin to focus on our recent work. The patient is silent in a household with distant parents who never spoke about feelings. I began to see that I was reacting to the material. I felt unrelated to the patient and realized that he was acting unrelated to me. The session proceeded. This state of experienced nonrelatedness continued for several months. I understood that an analytic process was present. Near the end of one session he described a movie that he had seen over the weekend that ended with the discovery by a boy of being sexually abused as a child. With this communication, I felt reconnected to him. Following his associations, I understood that there was an improvement in his nonrelatedness and self-numbness that had served as a defense against exposure and humiliation with an insufficient affect of safety. I connected his experience with a need to keep secrets within his family. Feeling unrelated, fragmented, and numb enforced his need to be secretive. For the next several sessions, the experience of relatedness, openness, and effectance were expressed in the material.

A rich body of knowledge about the self has become available from several psychoanalytic sources on infant development: infant research, a contemporary interpretation of Bowlby's (1986) work, and attachment theory. These sources can be used in conceptualizing clinical experiences related to the self such as self-experience, self as agency, and relatedness. Of course, the clinical situation is not infant development, but the hypotheses generated from infant development can serve as a platform that illuminates the self.

Infant researchers have shown that contrary to the original psychoanalytic description of the infant who is self-contained and quiescent until aroused by the demands of the drives, principally the oral drive, the infant is born seeking stimulation and engagement. Infant researchers have demonstrated that through the interaction between the infant and mother in which each seeks stimulation from the other the infant is regulated and begins to develop a capacity for self-regulation.

Development of a self and the dawn of awareness begin to evolve out of the infant–mother dyad. Stern (1985) describes the evolving self as continuous through layering, not stages that are achieved and left behind. He suggests that problems in the developmental layering of the self contribute to the development of psychopathology and can be considered in clinical material.

Attachment theory has evolved from Bowlby's original developmental and research model. The theory is based on an evolutionary affectionate bond between the infant and the mother which assists in understanding the infant–mother relationship. The qualities of the infant–mother bond influence the infant's affect regulation. Unmanageable threats from a rejecting, inconsistent, or traumatizing mother can result in defensive functioning. Defensive functioning initiated by problems of attachment differs from defense initiation that results from the pressure of unmanageable affects or impulses (Diamond and Blatt, 1999).

Actually, the findings of infant research support some of the basic hypotheses of object relations theory. Fairbairn (1952) hypothesizes that object seeking is the source of human motivation. The child withdraws from engagement with an object when the relationship is threatened. Winnicott (1958) writes that the self evolves from the duality of mother and child. Kleinians believe that the safety of the object tames the aggression of the infant. Sandler was well versed in both objects relations theory and Kleinian psychology. He placed affect in the center of the clinical situation, modulated by an affect of safety that promotes adaptation to the external world.

Sandler and Sandler (1978) found that within the past unconscious we see an object-related child within the adult. Both reality and fantasy are far more complex and interpersonal than can be described in terms of the cathexis of object with instinctual drive energy. I understand the Sandlers to mean that within the past unconscious lies the entire experience of the child, his representational world and cognition, sense of self, self as agency, wholeness, and relatedness. The entirety of the subjective experience of the developing child can be included in the transference and resistance.

Let's return to Stern's observation of the self as comprised of a developmental layering from immature to mature, leading to the attainment of self-cohesion, relatedness, and agency. The less mature components of this layering in the evolution of a self can be used as a defense that is characteristic of the child within the adult. The patient and I were experiencing a fragmented, nonrelated self-experience in a transference–countertransference dyad that originated in the past unconscious and was expressed through the present unconscious by means of the transference and contertransference. Our experiences appeared unchanged over several months. Finally, within the course of a session, a newer level of organization became apparent as he felt safe enough to express material related to his sexual abuse. The fragmented and nonrelated states disappeared. We felt more connected.

The findings of fragmented self and nonrelatedness are considered earlier layers of self-development that are used as a defense. It is as if the patient is saying, "I avoid seeing what I see by using a fragmented self, immature agency, and related self instead of a whole functioning self. I am protected against a more open self that is vulnerable to overwhelming affect and exposure of my secrets."

The patient was expressing aspects of the child within the adult who had to protect himself—with a fragmented nonrelated self—against humiliation and embarrassment without an affect of safety. I reacted to the transference with a countertransference reaction that also included the defense of a fragmented, nonrelated, numb self. Only when the patient could tell his story more directly did the fragmented, nonrelated, numbed self become more contained. For this to happen, we both had to integrate our individual stories so that they could be remembered rather than repeated. The patient worked to understand and integrate the transference, and I had to understand and integrate my countertransference to achieve an affect of safety against humiliation and shame to implement the ideal of "promoting the analysis to the last consequence." Metaphorically, I was "directed to removing all resistances" to enable the patient to tell her story. We were transforming our stories, which were expressed in the repetition compulsion, into memories that can be experienced in a state of wholeness with more passivity and vulnerability.

As the analysis progressed, the use of the representational world helped in following my patient and my experiences as he elaborated more of his story, which included his rage, sexuality, and traumatic experiences of abuse and neglect in the form of conflict and transference. He began one of our sessions by describing a dream. He was lying in a bed, and his father was coming up the stairs. A big snake was in his bed. He said that he understood that the dream had to do with sex, a large penis, and a priest who was a friend of the family. He began crying because he could not believe that anything like that happened. He said he knew that he grew up frightened about everything. He never stood up for himself. His family lived with secrets. No one spoke out. I felt that the analysis was progressing as more details of his sexual abuse were brought out.

The next session began with his saying that he had not felt like coming and had nothing to say. The session was filled with silence. When I suggested that his reaction was a response to the previous session, he responded with more silence. After this session, he began arriving late and complaining that he no longer felt like coming. He was critical of my lack of understanding and felt that he had made little progress. This session began a long period of his analysis in which the quality of the sessions changed from an evolving progression of material with the elaboration of the themes to a regression with a manifest absence of new material. It could have been described as a period of intense resistance. I still felt intimately connected to him, but in a sadomasochistic relationship. It appeared that there was very little I could say that was acceptable. I became frustrated and angry. I had anticipated progressing to greater clarity about the suggested sexual abuse by a priest, but instead this theme disappeared, and he frustrated me by withholding.

During this period, he described a dream of going somewhere with dangerous dogs. He said that he had been reading a book about a mother and daughter who were kidnaped. The mother was killed, and the daughter was raped. My patient said that he had awoken the day before the dream feeling sexy, but by the time he went to bed that night, his amorous feelings had disappeared. He continued to complain that I was unable to help him get over his depression.

I began interpreting components of his representational world—that is, the sadomasochism as superego introjects, the enormous guilt that he was living out with me, and the absence of any other affect outside the sadomasochism. I told him that it appeared that his inner world of experiences was a safe haven for him against the helplessness of being alone and abused without anyone to help him. During subsequent sessions, I noted the projective identification components of his frustration and anger with my frustration and anger that fused our relationship. I also recognized her intense masochism and the amount of self-punishment that he was enduring.

I was using concepts of his representational world, the object relations infused with intense affects of aggression and narcissism that represented part of the child within. This material was the story that he could not tell, a story that began in his past unconscious and passed into the present unconscious in the form of transferences, but was impeded in passing from the present unconscious and the external world because of the anticipation of too much humiliation, embarrassment, and lack of sufficient safety. The recognition of the incongruity between his lack of safety and the safety that was actually present because of our relationship and my interventions enabled the analysis to progress.

After considerable working through of his early traumas, especially his sexual abuse, the transference resistance shifted from details of the content of his sadomasochistic memories and fantasies with distant parents to the lack of availability of anyone safe to listen to his story. In the transference resistance during this phase, he was saying, "I am more in touch with the memories and fantasies of what happened to me. I feel them as mine, but there is an aspect of my experience that there is no one to safely tell my story to which leaves me isolated with a need to turn inward. I need to communicate in some creative fashion if I am to know that these experiences comprise my self." This transference resistance rests on the border of the third box, consciousness, and the external world.

Sandler's contributions to psychoanalysis took place during an era of transition in psychoanalysis from clinical work. The depolarization and plurality in psychoanalytic positions that Sandler was instrumental in initiating prompted analysts to look to basic clinical concepts and techniques to guide their observations and only secondly to use a variety of theories to embellish their clinical understanding of the psychoanalytic situation.

Assuming that the goal of psychoanalysis is enabling the patient to become familiar with the child within that is repeated in the transference, the analyst has considerable flexibility to use a variety of theories to make the clinical data more coherent and meaningful. This subjective and experiential perspective, which rests on an experiencing self that is an agency, is the entry into clinical work. This perspective enables the patient and analyst to follow the closeness, empathy, and humanness of the clinical situation while also following the derivatives of the drives, structures, energy, and object relations within the clinical material.

REFERENCES

Behrends, R. S. & Blatt, S. J. (1985), Internalization and psychological development throughout the life cycle. *The Psychoanalytic Study of the Child,* 40:11–39. New Haven, CT: Yale University Press.

Bowlby, J. (1986), *Loss, Sadness, and Depression.* New York: Basic Books.
Diamond, D. & Blatt, S. J. (1999), Prologue. *Psychoanal. Inq.,* 19:424–447.
Fairbairn, W. R. D. (1952), *Psychoanalytic Studies of Personality.* London: Tavistock.
Gill, M. & Holtzman, P. S. (1976), Essays in memory of George Klein. In: *Psychology Versus Metapsychology. Psychological Issues,* Monogr. 36. New York: International Universities Press.
Greenberg, J. R. & Mitchell, S. A. (1983), *Object Relations in Psychoanalytic Theory.* Cambridge, MA: Harvard University Press.
Guntrip, H. (1971), *Psychoanalytic Theory, Therapy, and the Self.* New York: Basic Books.
Holt, R. (1975), The past and future of ego psychology. *Psychoanal. Quart.,* 44: 550–576.
Klein, G. S. (1976), *Psychoanalytic Theory: An Exploration of Essentials.* New York: International Universities Press.
Lichtenberg, J. (1989), *Psychoanalysis and Motivation.* Hillsdale, NJ: The Analytic Press.
Loewald, H. (1960), On the therapeutic action of psychoanalysis. *Internat. J. Psycho-Anal.,* 41:16–33.
Meissner, W. (1986), Some notes on Hartmann's ego psychology and the psychology of the self. *Psychoanal. Inq.,* 6:499–522.
Modell, A. (1993), *The Private Self.* Cambridge, MA: Harvard University Press.
Peterfreund, E. (1973), On information processing models for mental phenomena. *Internat. J. Psycho-Anal.,* 54:351–357.
Rapaport, D. (1944), The scientific methodology of psychoanalysis. In: *The Collected Papers of David Rapaport.* New York: Basic Books, 1967.
Sandler, J. (1987), *From Safety to Superego.* London: Karnac Books.
_______ & Sandler, A.-M. (1978), On the development of object relations and affects. *Internat. J. Psycho-Anal.,* 59:285–296.
_______ & _______ (1984), The past unconscious, the present unconscious, and interpretation of the transference. *Psychoanal. Inq.,* 4:367–399.
Stern, D. (1985), *The Interpersonal World of the Infant: A View from Psychoanalysis and Developmental Psychology.* New York: Basic Books.
Stolorow, R. D. (1978), The concept of psychic structure: Its metapsychologic and clinical psychoanalytic meanings. *Internat. Rev. Psycho-Anal.,* 5:313–320.
Stone, L. (1961), *The Psychoanalytic Situation.* New York: International Universities Press.
Strachey, J. (1957), Editor's note—On narcissism: An introduction. *Standard Edition,* 14:69–71. London: Hogarth Press, 1957.
_______ (1961), Editor's note—The ego and the id. *Standard Edition,* 19:3–11. London: Hogarth Press, 1961.
Wallerstein, R. S. (1992), *Common Ground of Psychoanalysis.* Northvale, NJ: Aronson.
Winnicott, W. D. (1958), *Through Paediatrics to Psychoanalysis: Collected Papers.* New York: Brunner/Mazel.

626 Purdy Street
Birmingham, MI 48009
bornsteinm@cs.com

Working with Sandler's Theories

HENRY F. SMITH, M.D.

My contribution to this issue of *Psychoanalytic Inquiry* highlights not only Sandler's prodigious successes but also those aspects of his work that remain ambiguous. These uncertainties derive in part from his effort to integrate different frames of reference in his conceptualizations. The bits of theory that clinicians actually use in the consulting room tend to simplify, revise, and even contradict the more complex theories Sandler developed. Some of Sandler's proposals may be seen as reframings of earlier theory at different levels of abstraction, and hence more compatible with them than generally acknowledged. I note the inclusion of Kleinian strains, which Sandler legitimized for non-Kleinian analysts, and conclude with a consideration of the "identity of perception" as a fundamental aspect of cognition and a territory yet to be fully explored.

THE DISCUSSANT OF A SERIES OF PAPERS HONORING A REVERED analyst is in an awkward position. He can join in the celebration, and add little to the discourse; he can critique the celebrants and the celebratee, and risk being a spoilsport; or he can do a bit of both, which is the path I will try to follow. I am reminded of a memorial meeting held by loving disciples of Elvin Semrad in Boston shortly after his death in 1977. Harold Searles was the discussant. With a

Henry F. Smith, M.D. is Editor, *The Psychoanalytic Quarterly;* Training and Supervising Analyst, Psychoanalytic Institute of New England, East (PINE); Member, Boston Psychoanalytic Society and Institute.

backward glance at the enormous photograph of Semrad projected on the wall behind the speakers, he warned of the dangers of canonization, both for the canonizers and for the memory of the one being canonized. President Kennedy, no stranger himself to idealization, commented similarly that the risk to the truth is not the lie but the myth.

I do not think I am adding to that risk if I say that when Joseph Sandler died prematurely on October 6, 1998, a palpable shudder could be felt throughout the psychoanalytic world. It was unlike any other such moment I have known in our small professional universe, more like the death of a president or head of state.

My own relationship with him was limited to professional events, but I came to know him well enough to grasp the depth of his thinking, the encouragement he gave to others, and his sense of humor. A few years after finishing my training, I chaired a panel on which he was presenting a paper. He had just been elected President of the International Psychoanalytical Association. I can still hear his voice when I called him in London, anxious to see his presentation before I wrote my introduction. Gently but firmly he confessed, "I'm a bit overwhelmed these days." When we finally spoke a few minutes before the panel, we sat behind the curtains in the lobby of the Waldorf and gossiped, he telling me with a wry smile about Anna Freud's role as a matchmaker for many of her students, including, as it turned out, my own analyst. Rich diet for a recent graduate.

But it was his scholarly dedication that had been part of the world as I knew it. At the time of my psychiatric training in the early 1970s he seemed to be one of the pillars of the known theoretical universe. In the years since then, he consolidated his presence and importance in country after country around the world in a way that few other such figures in our field have done. When he died, I realized that in a more personal way he had become one of that small group of figures—representations to be sure—who were supposed to be there forever.

There are certain respects in which Sandler's work is even more pertinent today than when it was written. It was not so long ago that different schools of analysis had only two ways of dealing with one another. They could either fight bitterly or disavow the other's presence. Only recently have we begun to wonder if we indeed share common ground, as Wallerstein (1988, 1990) put it, and, if so, where that ground may lie (Smith, 2003a). Our ability to think in these terms is partly a result of Sandler's integrative efforts, and in this era of psychoanalytic plurality we would do well to examine those efforts rather closely, both for his successes and his failures.

My own sense is that Sandler had several theoretical goals, though not always explicit ones: first, to make our theory—or at least that particular version of drive and ego psychology he inherited—more clinically verifiable and usable; second, as a number of the authors in this volume have pointed out, to reconcile psychoanalytic theory with his own research data and the findings of the neighboring cognitive sciences; third, to explore our various preconscious theories and to make them as conscious and explicit as possible; and fourth, to integrate different theoretical conceptions when possible and, when impossible, to acknowledge the useful coexistence of competing and sometimes contradictory frames of reference. As an example of the latter, we might think of Sandler's own lifelong loyalty to the topographic theory, with which he constantly tinkered, elaborating it, updating it, adding compartments to it, all the while maintaining it side by side with structural and object relational conceptualizations.

Sandler was not alone in his effort to sharpen the clinical focus of theory. All schools of analysis have tried in recent decades to make their theories more clinically immediate. We can see it on this side of the Atlantic in the late evolution of ego psychology: Paul Gray's (1986) focus on the clinical "surface," for example, and Brenner's (1982, 1994, 2002) attention to compromises between clinically observable wishes, defenses, and self-punitive trends. As Holder notes in his paper in this volume, the distinction Sandler drew between the nonexperiential world of internal objects and the experiential world of the derivatives of those objects parallels the distinction between drives and drive derivatives, and this latter distinction forms much of the basis of Brenner's shift away from the abstract agencies of the mind. And we can see these trends in Sandler's own backyard in the extraordinary attention the contemporary British Kleinians pay to clinical interaction in the transference and countertransference.

While several of the authors in this volume make clear the overlap between Sandler's positions and their own, for the most part they do not underscore the similarities between his views and those of other competing psychoanalytic approaches, perhaps in deference to Sandler's wish to provide a corrective for what he regarded as the excesses of the other perspectives, including those Kleinian and ego-psychological positions with which he in fact shared many overlapping points of view. If Sandler's explorations of counter-transference and role responsiveness are, as many have pointed out, a response to the Kleinian methods and theories that surrounded him—including his wish, as Gabbard suggests, to make peace with his neighbor, Betty Joseph—is it too much to consider that the shift we have seen over the last two decades in contemporary British Kleinian methodologies may have been partly a result of Sandler's attention to and attempt to understand the phenomenology of their methods, theories, and observations, and his own critiques of their overinclusiveness?

Sandler is also not alone in his integrative efforts. I think here of Andre Green, diagramming the different contemporary theoretical branches in psychoanalysis, and, in a synthetic tour de force, locating them all on the original Freudian tree, or Leo Rangell's (1988) commitment to "total composite psychoanalytic theory." But such integrations are easier to construct if we keep the focus somewhat nonspecific. Sandler's struggles with the *details* of different aspects of theory reveal both the conceptual weaknesses as well as the strengths of the integrative process.

In reading even a portion of his immense bibliography, one wonders if Sandler might at one time have wanted to write a definitive or unifying theory, one that would bring together all our psychoanalytic frames of reference, but, as time passed, he ran into insoluble contradictions, unanswerable questions, and his own changing interests.

There are, to be sure, other ways to understand Sandler's approach to psychoanalysis. Like both Anna and Sigmund Freud—and in keeping with the concept of persistence he championed—Sandler was unwilling to let any piece of theory go, if it might prove useful. While this lent a richness and complexity to his theorizing, it inevitably left a number of unsettled areas. In acknowledgment of this on a personal level, Sandler (1983) assessed the particular clutter that inhabits the preconscious mind of many psychoanalysts, where different theories or part-theories exist in happy contradiction with each other, as long as they are not forced into the same daylight space. He saw this as a given for all, and, while some have disputed this assumption, his observations have proven generative to a number of clinical investigators examining the analyst's mind at work, notably Vicki Hamilton's (1996) important study of preconscious processes in the analyst. I would only add that, while many of us can attest in our own work to the more conscious manifestations of the clutter Sandler recognized, we need to leave room for the possibility that some analysts have tidier minds than others, and for the enormous variations in the location and prominence of theory in the clinical thinking of different analysts (Smith, 2003c).

Whatever Sandler's motivations in all this, such efforts inevitably raise the question of how one can combine observations from different frames of reference without creating an unlawful mix of levels of abstraction and the "hybrid concepts" (Slap and Levine, 1978) that inevitably result. If I have one criticism of this volume as a whole it is that the contributors tend to speak only of Sandler's prodigious successes and not the imperfections, nor the work yet to be done. While he would have been pleased with this tribute, I suspect it might also have puzzled him slightly, as he was himself so used to questioning, reexamining, and reworking the rough edges of his and others' models. In fact, I would suggest that it is this quality of mind that eventually proved so generative, namely that he wrote as he thought, and as we read his writing, we can hear him thinking.

I would now like to turn to a more detailed look at the individual papers in this commemorative issue, with an eye to how each of the contributors manages the dilemmas in Sandler's writing. As I understand their task, the authors have been asked to consider three of Sandler's major contributions, the representational world, the background of safety, and the concept of role responsiveness, represented in the main by the three seminal papers that bear the names of these concepts. All six articles present particularly clear elucidations of Sandler's work in regard to one or more of his preoccupations, stressing the linkages with their own points of view, and thereby rendering both Sandler's views and their own more accessible. In that sense, each fulfills his task admirably. While all six authors provide useful and important consolidations, in my view, they also make Sandler's work as a whole appear more cohesive than it may in fact have been, something that is easier to do if one looks at the body of his work from a distance, at a level of generalization considerably greater than the one in which he immersed himself in its creation. The exception is Alex Holder, who, because he grapples with some of the more puzzling details of Sandler's theory, rather than focusing so much on an overview, usefully reveals ambiguities in Sandler's thinking, and for this we are extremely grateful.

The Representational World

In my view Sandler's description of the representational world has been one of his major successes—perhaps the most successful integrative effort we have seen in psychoanalysis, bridging, as it does, what we observe clinically with what can be inferred from research studies, thus bringing the psychoanalytic world together with a cognitive Piagetian one. The concept grew in part out of Sandler's wish to find a link between the intrapsychic focus of classical theory and the conceptual schema of object relational approaches. To oversimplify: in Sandler's (1962) original model, the intrapsychic world of the developing child could be viewed on a kind of inner stage on which there appeared various and changing representations of self and others; thus, as the analyst's attention shifted back and forth between drive-derived and object relational conceptualizations, he or she could maintain a common intrapsychic point of focus within the mind of the patient. That focal point would include the patient's conscious and unconscious *wishes* of both instinctual and, Sandler would add, noninstinctual origin, such that every wish included a self-representation, an object representation, and a representation of the interaction between those same self- and object representations. We can detect Sandler's effort in this conceptualization to try to make sense of certain Kleinian conceptualizations and to bring them in line with the theories on which he was raised, with the Hampstead index he helped to develop, and with his own clinical observations.

Fonagy's masterful summary of Sandler's work is further testimony to the remarkable generativity of this piece of Sandler's theoretical creations, particularly within the British Society. Fonagy's own work on mentalization, one of the most important in our current psychoanalytic landscape, seems an effort to document the establishment of the representational world itself, which is to carry out in developmental studies what Sandler began, and to translate them ultimately into technical recommendations. We need only look at Fonagy's discussions elsewhere of clinical phenomena, such as "mirroring," to see that he is delineating an aspect of therapeutic action, derived from developmental observations, that applies to all technical approaches and in that sense may lead us to a final common pathway for certain aspects of therapeutic action (Fonagy et al., 2002).

As I have already suggested, Holder, one of Sandler's important collaborators, applies the analytical tools they developed together for their highly influential short volume (Sandler, Dare, and Holder, 1973), *The Analyst and the Patient,* in examining some thorny details of Sandler's descriptive theory; in so doing he reveals the complexity of the man's thinking, and some of what remains confusing. As a window into aspects of Sandler's work, I will focus for a moment on one of Sandler's explications that Holder highlights for us.

Consider Sandler's effort to deconstruct projective identification in light of his theory of representations. In his paper on the concept of projective identification, Sandler (1987) defines three types of projective identification, beginning with what he calls "first-stage projective identification," illustrated by the intrapsychic defensive process Melanie Klein initially outlined. Noting that historically many authors began to link the concepts of countertransference and projective identification, Sandler designates the resultant altered concept that includes the analyst's participation in the process "second- stage projective identification." As an illustration of this version of the concept, Sandler cites Racker's (1968) views on concordant and complementary identification. Racker defined concordant identification as the identification of the analyst's id, ego, and superego with the patient's id, ego, and superego, respectively, and considered it the result of simple empathic identification. Complementary identification was a term Racker borrowed from Helene Deutsch (1926) to describe, as Racker put it, the analyst's identification with the patient's internal objects. Sandler, however, makes a subtle but highly significant adjustment in his understanding of both of these phenomena, suggesting that the analyst's identification in each case is with the patient's self- or object representation in the patient's unconscious fantasies. He goes on to designate as "third-stage projective identification" the concept of projective identification as articulated by Bion (see Grinberg, Sor, and Bianchedi, 1977), wherein, as Sandler viewed it, the process is no longer occurring in fantasy but rather the projections are apparently made directly into the external object, a conceptual view about which Sandler had serious reservations.

Having clarified these three conceptualizations of projective identification, Sandler then returns to the "second-stage" type and suggests, as Holder puts it, that the "analyst's shift from a complementary identification (with the fantasied object representation) to a concordant identification (with the self-representation) in the countertransference corresponds to two distinct steps in a patient's intrapsychic employment of projective identification." And here Holder quotes Sandler (1987):

> Countertransference response due to second-stage projective identification is *always* based on identification with a fantasy object, and when it appears to be identification with aspects of the self-representation, a further intrapsychic step has occurred in the patient's fantasying process; that is, *a further projective identification* has taken place into a new fantasy analyst-object which then contains projected aspects of the self [p. 23].

This is a moment in which we can hear Sandler thinking through a piece of clinical theory, and, as with any fresh thinking, leaving some ambiguities in his wake. It is an example of what I have been referring to as the richness and complexity of his thinking, for in trying to extend our understanding both of the patient's intrapsychic processes and the analyst's participation in them, Sandler introduces us to a level of detail that is at once illuminating, and at the same time a bit problematic. For starters, it is not entirely clear what he means.

Because he has just used *concordant identification* as one illustration of second-stage projective identification, Sandler seems to suggest that in all cases of concordant identification the analyst, appearing to identify with the fantasied self-representation of the patient, in fact identifies with the fantasied object representation of the patient into which the patient has projected aspects of his or her self-representation. This would lead us to the intriguing conclusion that, given the ubiquity of projective identification, all identifications are fundamentally identifications with object representations, which may secondarily contain "projected aspects of the self." On the other hand, although it would seem to contradict what he has just established, Sandler might be leaving room for other sorts of concordant identifications not "based on second-stage projective identification." The distinction is important because of the point Holder ultimately makes. But before we get to that, we should note that either reading of this passage represents a disagreement on Sandler's part with Racker.

Holder seems to feel that Sandler means the former: "If I read Sandler correctly, he is suggesting that, in a concordant identification, the analyst, in his countertransference, is identifying with those parts of the self-representation which the patient has projected into the fantasy object." But then Holder himself makes room for the latter: "If this is correct, such identifications would have to be distinguished from the analyst's temporary identification with a patient's self-representations which are not projected into object representations. It is obvious that such empathic identifications form a constant element in our daily clinical work." In so saying, Holder rescues the simple clinical notion of trial identification from the complexity of Sandler's phenomenology and returns us to Racker's simpler view in which concordant identifications are more or less equated with empathy.

Holder's intervention here is noteworthy because it suggests that the everyday notions we use in clinical work may be of a different order from the complexity of the theory Sandler was evolving. Notice that the level of clinical theory Holder reasserts is not so different from the simpler Bionian and Kleinian views of projective identification against which Sandler was arguing, raising the question that, however useful the complex analyses of the sort Sandler has undertaken may be in helping us to understand processes underlying our work, as clinicians, rather than as theoreticians, we may need simpler rules of thumb in the consulting room, even as our more sophisticated theories expose the inaccuracy of those simplifications.

For here we need to ask: Is Holder's rescue attempt consistent with what Sandler had in mind or with the specificity of Sandler's theory? If, as Holder seems to maintain, Sandler views all concordant identifications as identifications with the patient's object representations, and if, as Racker suggests, those same concordant identifications are what we mean by empathy, then we would have to take Sandler at his word that even simple empathic trial identifications, no less than extended ones, must be viewed as identifications with object representations, disguised as self-representations, or with some inevitable mix of the two. Setting aside for the moment the question as to whether there can be any representation that is not a mixture of self and object, or self with object, or any representations that, as fantasies, are not in themselves defensive structures, I suggest that, even if we limit ourselves to Sandler's representational theory, the situation may in fact be even more complex than the one I have just outlined.

Notice that in all of this discussion of projective identification, Sandler's primary interest is in the *analyst's* identifications, rather than the patient's, much as Racker's was. This is the "second stage" Sandler has in mind, and it is the area of projective identification that preoccupied him for several decades, one he repeatedly tried to clarify, as, for example, in his discussion of role responsiveness. But if one follows Sandler's reasoning about fantasy and the representational world carefully—and it is a position I firmly support—we have to take into account the analyst's own representational world. And when we add the analyst's representational world to the mix, it leads us to the conclusion that, in identifying with the patient's fantasy of an object representation, the analyst, too, is in fact identifying with a fantasy of his or her own making, not being able to perceive the patient's fantasy directly. How could there ever be a direct identification with the patient's fantasy any more than there could be a direct projection into the external object of the analyst? Listen to Schafer (1968) on this point, "It is important to adhere strictly to the proposition that identification takes place not with a person but with one or more representations of that person. The subject's [i.e., in this case, the analyst's] conception and experience of the other person is only one possible version of him" (p. 142). In other words, putting all this together, the process of projective identification takes place solidly in the realm of fantasy, specifically the patient's fantasy of an object representation (or more accurately a mix of self- and object representations) that the patient projects and to which the analyst responds, producing a representational fantasy of his or her own making with which the analyst identifies. If we add to this mix the exchanges of fantasies—through projection and identification—unfolding at all times between patient and analyst, the result becomes very complex indeed, and this complexity, I suggest, accurately depicts the analytic situation.

To summarize, Sandler has moved us here from the simple, or, in his view, simplistic, notion that the patient projects into the analyst and the analyst identifies with that projection or with the patient, to the notion that the analyst identifies with the patient's self-representation, which, he notes, is itself a fantasy on the patient's part, and he has then added that in second-stage projective identification, when the analyst identifies with the patient self-representation, he is actually identifying with the patient's object representation into which the patient has projected aspects of himself, and, finally, in Sandler's absence, we add that all of the analyst's identifications are in fact with his or her own fantasies of the patient's representational world, in which fantasies of self- and object representations always appear in combinations of the two and never as isolated entities.

Sandler's analysis of the phenomenon of concordant identification is an example of what Michels (2003) has recently called process theory, as opposed to content theory. I further distinguish here between the evolution of process theory and the use of simplified, and perhaps even falsified, versions of that theory in the consulting room, for, as Holder's "rescue operation" implies, the details of such theories may be too rich for the clinician's blood and some simpler working notions or metaphors may be all he or she can manage in the clinical moment. There are many such notions with which we stabilize ourselves in the interaction with the patient, and none of them strictly fit what we know to be going on. "Defense before drive," an idea so useful for many years, makes little sense theoretically if all defenses are inseparable from the wishful, defensive, self-punitive compromise formations into which they are bound. "Interpret from the surface," surely a holdover from the topographic model, continues to curry favor even among those adherents to structural theory who have tried to eliminate the last vestiges of the topographic theory from their work. Similarly, such notions as "The patient has put this into me and I need to contain it" or "I am one with the patient" may lead the analyst to effective and sophisticated clinical activity, even though they are quite impossible to take as literal representations of the phenomena that are occurring, and this was Sandler's point.

I have tried to illustrate the ways clinicians use various bits of theory elsewhere (Smith, 2001), and, as we shall see, the clinical illustrations in this volume provide yet further evidence of the ways a particular theory or part-theory can provide a framework and direction without the analyst's having to keep in mind the entire theoretical structure. Thus, however usefully and relentlessly Sandler's and

Schafer's deliberations on the domain of the patient's and the analyst's fantasy life keep us focused on the psychical nature of the reality we are investigating, in the heat of the clinical moment we rely on simpler rubrics. (For a description of the clinical experience of projective identification, see Spillius, 1992.)

Here we might keep in mind not only the difference between a theory and how it is used, but also the ways in which any theory operates on several different levels of abstraction simultaneously, and how these different levels or part-theories communicate with each other and with their practical applications. I suggest that as the clinician digests any given theory it undergoes various sorts of metabolic change until it lodges, consciously and preconsciously, in a clinically usable form, a working model of what was once a more complex edifice.

Gardner (1995) speaks to this point when he says he prefers a "theory that's simple enough to remember and complex enough to 'forget'" (p. 90), such as the familiar "three points on the compass" (Gardner, personal communication, 1986) of structural theory. Or when he decries the lack of attention we have given to developing theories suited to the "free-attending workings of the minds that will use those theories" (Gardner, 1991, p. 867). Gardner (1995) has also noted that however much practice lags behind theory, theory too lags behind practice: "as in any discipline . . . art, in the main, goes far ahead of theory and it's theory's job to try persistently to close the gap" (pp. 78–79), a view Sandler (1990) supported.

To be sure, in North America we are more accustomed to using relatively simple, practical, and empirically based working models, whether they be Gill's (1982) focus on the actuality of the transference, Schwaber's (1992) pursuit of the patient's vantage point, or Brenner's more elaborate but still minimalist theoretical positions. Compared to many European theoretical models, each of these might be said to be more adapted to the "workings of the minds that will use those theories," in Gardner's terms, than are their European counterparts. In my view this does not necessarily mean that these North American points of view oversimplify the work, nor that the European versions are too cumbersome, if modifed preconsciously by the intuitive clinician. One can, however, make a case that the sparseness of Brenner's particular model leads the clinician to vistas of increasing rather than decreasing complexity (Smith, 2003b). We have no way of testing at this point what sort of theory, simple or complex, or what use of theory, deliberate or intuitive, leads an analyst to a more successful outcome. Different analysts analyze differently, and different theories and part-theories shape the work in different ways. The contrast between theories that have evolved on either side of the Atlantic reflects in part the level of abstraction each culture favors.

Some of these conclusions are supported by the generous clinical examples provided by Cooper and Bornstein. Designed to illustrate the usefulness of Sandler's conceptualizations, they also underscore the way in which experienced clinicians use theory in the consulting room. It is often said that the best art is that which conceals itself; accordingly, it is difficult to see the operation of theory in the work of these master analysts. Both transcripts seem to me illustrations of solid analytic work, wherein Sandler's views, as he articulated them, are clearly pertinent but not necessarily essential. Many contemporary theoretical positions have built into them various reminders to keep the astute clinician "in the neighborhood" of the patient, as Busch (1992) has put it, and hence the success of an intervention can often be explained after the fact by any number of current theories. I am not suggesting that Bornstein and Cooper are *not* using Sandler in the way they say they are, but rather that the relationship between Sandler's theory and their clinical work is a relatively nonspecific one, the linkage not one-to-one. Moreover, I wonder if they—or someone else—might not achieve similar results by using a different set of assumptions, stemming from a different theoretical frame of reference.

Both clinicians would, I suspect, disagree with this hypothesis. Bornstein, for one, has suggested that it was Joseph and Anne-Marie Sandler's specific intent with the "three-box model" to "narrow the hiatus" between metapsychological theory and the clinical work that might stem from it. While this may indeed have been the effect, I am not convinced that, strictly speaking, it was where the Sandlers started. Rather, it seems to me that they were trying to anchor their own clinical observations in largely topographical terms, in order to provide a theoretical corrective for the technical missteps they observed others making. In so doing, one might argue that they were trying to solve at a metapsychological level certain technical problems that might more accurately be considered matters of clinical judgment. However useful their explanations may be, I wonder if, in reinforcing or buttressing their technical concerns with metapsychological analysis, they are not mixing levels of abstraction in a way that tends to confuse the status of the theory.

The Sandlers (1987) make clear their technical concerns when they write regarding the past unconscious and the present unconscious, "For some psychoanalysts the two are equated, and current material may be systematically interpreted as if (in our terms) the present unconscious was identical with the past unconscious" (p. 337). I suspect here they may have had in mind not only certain stereotypical Kleinian approaches, but also the heavy-handed application of some ego-psychological ones as well. As an alternative, however, and as an illustration of not collapsing clinical judgment into a metapsychological framework, I suggest that, if, from a structural point of view, we were to regard all clinical material as made up of wishes, past and present, defenses against those wishes, self-punishments for those wishes, and the misery those wishes evoke, it becomes much less clear what is past and what is present in the topographic form the Sandlers have maintained, *but that does not mean that past and present are equated nor that the past would need to be interpreted indiscriminately.* Rather it becomes a matter of clinical judgment to what extent the past is alive in the present and to what extent *either past or present* is accessible to the patient. For many patients the present unconscious may be no more accessible that the past unconscious, despite the fact that one might assume otherwise from a cursory reading of the Sandlers' schema.

The direct use of metapsychological observation in the clinical situation is more common in Europe than in North America, and, in keeping with this, the Sandlers were using higher level theory to make a more accurate and more effective technical "map" as they saw it, but I wonder if the two realms can be reconciled in such neat packages. However much both clinical observation and metapsychology may inform the clinician, each shaping the other, it is clearer in my view to maintain the two as distinct levels of discourse. I am not suggesting that metapsychology is any less important or less necessary to the clinical endeavor, as is frequently argued, nor that it does not infuse and shape the primary data, only that clinical theory and metapsychological theory describe the clinical situation at different levels of abstraction and generalization and to blur that distinction may lead to a lack of theoretical and clinical clarity.

The mixing of levels of abstraction to create hybrid concepts is something Joseph Sandler did quite deliberately when he wanted to render his theory less mechanical and less remote from the clinical data. I am thinking here of his use of the term *feeling cathexes,* quoted by Cooper.[1] I realize that it was in fact precisely to avoid the confusion of highly abstract concepts that Sandler shifted our focus to feelings and attitudes and away from more mechanistic terms such as energy distribution (Joffe and Sandler, 1967, p. 186) in the first place, but nonetheless feelings derive from one level of abstraction, the experiential, to use his phrase, and cathexis from another, the nonexperiential. To mix the two seems to me inherently conceptually confusing.

To belabor this point for a minute, the phrase feeling cathexis is itself ambiguous. Thinking of the term only in isolation we might ask, does it refer to those cathexes that are infused and driven by feelings, the feeling attached to a cathected object, for example, or does it refer to the person's investment or cathexis of a feeling per se, a feeling as the aim of the cathexis? We can assume from the context that Sandler means the former, but the confusion derives from the hybrid nature of the term feeling cathexis, and its analogy to the original economic use of the concept, as in object cathexis, wherein both halves of the phrase are on the same, nonexperiential level of abstraction, the object clearly the aim of the cathexis. It is worth noting that some of these inherent ambiguities in Sandler's theorizing, which one could argue stem from ambiguities in the field of observation itself, invite the very elasticity of the concepts that he worked hard to clarify and, at times, opposed.

In actual fact, the metapsychological aspects of the "three-box model" seem remote from Bornstein's clinical task. If Bornstein himself uses the model more as a metaphorical guide to focus on what is accessible and tolerable to the patient, a task, as I look at it, for which another model might prove equally useful, he introduces a bit of confusion relative to the third box. Bornstein states, accurately enough, "The third box contains consciousness that folds into the external world," and that "affects of humiliation, shame, and embarrassment are the gatekeepers of the border between the second and third

[1]See, for example, "self- and object representations receive an increasing abundance of *feeling cathexes* as development proceeds" (Sandler and Joffe, 1969, p. 253).

boxes." But subsequently he adds, "By following Sandler's model, one can see that the humiliation and embarrassment that is set at the border of the third box and reality is based upon the danger of narcissistic damage." Here it is unclear whether Bornstein is referring to the border between the second and third boxes, or some other border in between the "third box" and what he designates "reality." This is the sort of ambiguity that sets the reader to thinking. I assume Bornstein means the former, and that he has folded "reality" into the third box, along with consciousness. But reality was never so clearly confined in the Sandlers' (1983) original model. The very idea of enclosing reality within a box seems a contradiction in terms. Even consciousness is not so easy to contain, in recognition of which the Sandlers sometimes put consciousness in the "third box" and at others left the edges more fluid, as in their later 1987 paper, in which they simply located the present unconscious "at the border between the past unconscious and consciousness," leaving the latter open-ended. At any rate, the nature of the relationship between consciousness and what Bornstein calls "reality" is a critical one, not easily relegated to a single box, as he does, nor, I might add, fully addressed in Sandler's work.

The Background of Safety

It may be useful to view the conceptualizations that evolved from Sandler's early paper, "The Background of Safety," in the light of his lifelong interest in the role of affect in psychic life. Affect played a crucial role in his formulations of the representational world. First, Sandler viewed the child's earliest representations as affective ones; that is, distillates of early affective experience that he called *primary affective objects*. Over time, affect took its place at the heart of Sandler's theory of motivation, as Kernberg has pointed out, a view the two of them share within somewhat different frameworks.

As Sandler came to regard affect as the basic organizer and motivator of the psyche, he viewed representations as, variously, made up of affect, shaped by affect, and, in a sense, the source of affect. Thus, for example, the tension between an individual's actual self-representation at any given moment and his or her ideal self-representation (or ideal self, for short) could result in disappointment and diminished self-esteem. Sandler came to view this "representational discrepancy," as he called it, as the source of all psychic pain; and the "aim of all ego functioning" then became the reduction of such discrepancies in order to reestablish a "basic feeling state of well-being" (Joffe and Sandler, 1968, p. 229). We can see here Sandler's influence on later approaches to narcissism, notably self-psychological ones.

We can also see that the ego in Sandler's hands became a far more encompassing affect-monitor than it was in the ego psychology he inherited, now constantly reading the signals of both conscious and unconscious feeling-states. Thus, having struggled with Freud's first theory of anxiety, Sandler took on the second theory of anxiety, broadening the concept of signal anxiety to include all painful and pleasurable affects, both conscious and unconscious, in contrast to Freud's notion of signal anxiety as a solely unconscious intrapsychic event. We might ask, again, whether in so doing he simplified theory to fit clinical and developmental observations, or conflated fundamentally different clinical and conceptual domains.

Behind Sandler's interest in affect as a motivator, one can hear Freud's early interests in affect. Thus Sandler rejects the notion of affect as the signal for drive release, as depicted in the early Freud, a position that sets him somewhat apart from Kernberg, who retains some of this earlier formulation, despite the convergences in their views on motivation. And just as surely as Sandler rejects the early view of drive theory, he expands on the pleasure principle in "The Background of Safety," ultimately regarding the seeking of safety and security as a more fundamental need, one that could, as several of the authors in this volume attest, override the avoidance of pain. In other words, if Sandler initially saw the concept of safety as complementary to the avoidance of pain, he soon came to consider it preemptive.

But here we must ask, is this an example of one principle overriding another, or is it rather an illustration of the safety principle being pitted against a partial and somewhat archaic interpretation of the pleasure–unpleasure principle, in the fuller version of which the pursuit of safety might seem quite consistent with a person's effort to maximize pleasure and avoid pain. In other words, one could argue, using the pleasure–unpleasure principle as a guide, that the "pleasure" of safety, including the safety of familiar if deeply painful internal objects, might under certain circumstances outweigh the pain of a world without such objects or an objectless existence altogether. If one were to integrate an object relational view with the pleasure–unpleasure principle in this way, there would seem to be no contradiction between the two "principles," unless the pursuit of pleasure were interpreted so narrowly that it could not encompass such derivative motives as safety. Kernberg implies as much in his masterful integration and discussion of Sandler's ideas, when he describes the "affect of safety" as a "sublimatory aspect of libidinal relations (in contrast to sexual excitement as the most direct affective expression of libido)." So here I would ask: however useful an addition it may be, is Sandler's safety principle a competing conceptualization or simply a shift in terminology and level of abstraction? Notice the way he puts it in his initial paper on the topic, "In addition to directly defensive activity aimed at the reduction of anxiety, the ego will attempt to counterbalance the anxiety, so to speak, by heightening the safety level by whatever techniques it has at its disposal" (Sandler, 1960, p. 5). If we were to take a broad definition of defensive activity, such as Brenner's (1982) view that "every aspect of ego functioning can be and, at times, is used for defense" (p. 92), would there be any doubt that "defensive activity" and "heightening the safety level" become exact equivalents?

Here we must also consider the "elasticity," to use Sandler's term, his own concepts have undergone. It would appear, for example, that the safety principle has been widely interpreted to include many *conscious* forms of safety seeking, including the patient's conscious wish for a sense of safety in the analysis, in addition to the *unconscious* safety seeking with which Sandler began. Holder acknowledges this ambiguity implicitly when he tries to explain Sandler's use of the term "background feeling," noting that Sandler must have wanted "to convey that such feelings need not be conscious at all but can operate at a descriptively unconscious level." Clearly in Holder's mind, they can be either conscious or unconscious, but as the principle has come into widespread clinical use, the distinction between the two has become blurred.

Put another way, if it is a safety *principle* that overrides the pleasure–unpleasure *principle*, the two principles must at one time have been on the same metapsychological playing field or level of abstraction, part of the unconscious "nonexperiential" workings of the system, to use Sandler's terminology. There are practical reasons for my belaboring this point. As a principle at the *conscious* level, the elevation of the background of safety to an overriding concern is used to justify many forms of clinical activity on the part of the analyst, designed to make the patient *feel safe*. I am not suggesting that such technical maneuvers are *not* at times essential, but only that this is not where the principle began, and to elevate a principle of motivation to a principle of technique again blurs the distinction between the two realms in a way that may not be useful either clinically or theoretically. By contrast, in the old nomenclature, one would hardly speak of an analyst deliberately maximizing the patient's experience of unconscious pleasure, however much that might be a welcome (or not so welcome) by-product of the analysis and the analyst's approach.

To what extent Sandler intended to blur the distinction between the conscious and unconscious seeking of safety or to direct the analyst toward active work to ensure the patient's experience of safety is not clear, but in the current broadened use of the safety principle, one worries about the clinical simplifications it may encourage, or what may be left out of the clinician's thinking, designated as outside of conflict, for example, the sort of conflict, that is, that informs the pleasure–unpleasure principle in all of its complexity.

The complexity of the pursuit of safety would seem to be nowhere more important than with those patients we call masochistic that so bedeviled Freud, wherein the mix of erotic and aggressive wishes, defenses, self-punishments, along with the attachment to painful affect (Valenstein, 1973) and the catastrophic fear of aloneness and object loss, is not so clearly implied by the simple notion of safety. Ultimately, of course, it is not the terminology or the theory that is reductionistic, but the manner in which it is used.

From another theoretical point of view, however, it might also be useful to consider the experience of safety, conscious and unconscious, as itself a conflictual structure, shaped by these same aggressive and broadly defined erotic wishes, defenses, and self-punishments, rather than simply designating it a motivating principle, which tends to relegate the pursuit of safety to an unanalyzable given. I do not mean to eliminate principles of motivation altogether, nor to neglect a sense of "basic" safety that might be said to be essential to any analytic undertaking, only to suggest that as the patient's experience of safety becomes observable in the clinical situation, it should be subject to analysis.

I have the sense that at certain moments, either when he remained unsure, or when he was working on a concept that bridged several levels of consciousness (past and present—or unconscious, conscious, and preconscious), Sandler deliberately left the boundaries ambiguous. This may have reflected his own tolerance for the sort of theoretical ambiguity he noted in his 1983 paper, or he may not have wanted to imply more specificity than was possible at the time; but that ambiguity, necessary as it may be, invites the very conceptual drift he decried. In the natural course of things, if Sandler was always striving for greater specificity in his theories, each further venture inevitably introduced new complexities and revealed new ambiguities, as the details of his observations became subject to debate. If the result was puzzling and provocative at times, the same ambiguities that made it so stimulated further testing, verification, and research.

We cannot avoid noting that some of the elastic drift I have been outlining may have developed because of Sandler's own shifting theoretical, clinical, and political allegiances. This might apply in particular to those formulations like the safety principle that, rather than remaining complementary to the earlier ones he had inherited in his work with Anna Freud, eventually began to extrude them, including the drive theory in which they were embedded. Thus in 1960 he concluded his paper on the safety principle somewhat rashly, "Instinctual drives will always remain the prime motivators of behavior, and although I have, to use Freud's analogy, described a little part of the rider, this does not mean that the horse does not exist" (p. 8). Here he seems to be acknowledging the different and complementary levels on which he is working. However, four years after Anna Freud's death, Sandler (1983) would write definitively, "Not all unconscious wishes derive from the instinctual drives."

Taken as a group, the contributors to this issue hedge their bets on just how far along this path they locate their Sandler. Thus, Fonagy cites the later Sandler, who felt that "not all unconscious wishful fantasies could be traced back to sexual and aggressive instincts," effectively eliminating the drives as the basis for a general theory, whereas Gabbard cites a more conciliatory and earlier Sandler who judged "unconscious fantasy" to include "much more than simple derivatives of aggressive and libidinal drives," an argument that, depending on one's interpretation of the term *simple,* it might be difficult to find anyone to oppose.

On this point, it may be instructive to return to the comparison between Sandler and Brenner. Fonagy inadvertently brings the two into conjunction when he notes, "Sandler made explicit his conviction that the wish is the basic unit of psychoanalytic discourse," which could as easily be said of Brenner, or when he notes that Sandler "showed that the superego contains approving and permissive, as well as prohibiting figures," which mirror, in object relational terms, Brenner's formulation of the superego as made up of set of compromise formations, with loving as well as aggressive wishes, defenses, and prohibiting influences all in one.

In this light, I wonder why, in broadening our understanding of the mind, it was ultimately necessary for Sandler to discard the old rather than enlarge upon it. In his more moderate position Sandler (1983) wrote, "It is a gross mistake to regard the externalization of inner object relationships . . . as simply the direct or indirect fulfillment of unconscious instinctual wishes" (p. 43). While the operative word, once again, is "simply," Sandler would seem to be calling our attention here to the many layers inherent in the externalization of internalized object relations, opposing reductionistic interpretive strategies that could be falsely tied to such a theory. We see his concern with reductionism more directly when he writes, "It would be a great error, both clinically and theoretically, to equate [the impulse to cling] automatically with an oral instinctual wish" (Sandler, 1983, p. 42). If he has in mind an analyst who would move directly to such an interpretation, one would have to agree—and vehemently. But it remains unclear how relevant his caution is to a more contemporary view of conflict theory. Notice that Sandler is arguing here against an archaic form of drive theory, based on an early, linear view of psychosexual development, and opposing the approaches that might result from a direct translation of them into practice.

The contrast between Sandler and Brenner is sharpest, of course, when Sandler uses his concept of the present and past unconscious to suggest a kind of line in the theoretical sand, namely that there may be wishes in the present unconscious that are *not* drive derivatives, for example, whereas Brenner would regard the very terms *wish* and *drive derivative* as synonyms. More subtly, when Sandler (1983) writes, "Such an interaction may satisfy instinctual needs, but (at least equally) satisfies needs for security and familiarity" (p. 43), he suggests, again, that security, familiarity, and safety are not drive-derived, rather than considering that they may be complementary descriptions of the same need at different levels of abstraction.

Holder gets entangled in this quandary when he writes:

> From a contemporary point of view, it seems obvious that the intrapsychic representation of object relationships are not solely determined by instinctual drive wishes . . . it is rather the overall quality of the emotional relationship between an infant and his caregiver and its internalization as part of the representational world which is of crucial importance for growth and development.

No one would dispute the importance of the "overall quality" of such relationships, but it is unclear why they should be pitted against wishes of instinctual origin, as if the two were mutually exclusive, rather than codeterminants of both development and intrapsychic life.

What I am calling an archaic version of drive theory, against which Sandler seems to be arguing, may be a reflection of a theory of drives that is embedded in the topographic model. If so, Sandler's allegiance to topography may itself be partly responsible for keeping his argument with drive theory alive. Holder inadvertently alerts us to this possibility when he argues that the safety principle "inhibits the activation of the instinctual drives," a view of drive activity that I would suggest is based on an early and archaic Freudian model.

Before closing this section, we might note that Sandler was not above broadening certain concepts on his own, especially ones derived from a more strictly drive-oriented theory. I am thinking of the well-known comment in his seminal paper on role responsiveness which Gabbard quotes:

> I want to suggest that very often the irrational response of the analyst, which his professional conscience leads him to see entirely as a blind spot of his own, may sometimes be usefully regarded as a compromise formation between his own tendencies and his reflexive acceptance of the role which the patient is forcing on him.

It must have been with a bit of mischief that Sandler used the term compromise formation to designate the interactive (projective and introjective) phenomenon he was describing, rather than reserving the term for its original usage to denote a purely intrapsychic entity.

Role Responsiveness

I suspect it would and probably did surprise Sandler to discover that his slight paper on "Countertransference and Role Responsiveness," written for a symposium at the British Society in the casual tone of an afterthought, is among the most frequently cited articles in his bibliography. Clearly it was the right idea at the right time, anticipating as it did our more recent, and some would say interminable, focus on interaction and enactment.

Gabbard gives us a very clear summary of Sandler's broader views on countertransference, linking them with his own 1995 position on the emerging common ground of countertransference. Gabbard notes that when Sandler published this paper, "he felt that the classic view of transference as a displacement from the patient's libidinal or aggressive energic cathexis from a past object to the person of the analyst was an inadequate and archaic explanation of what happened in the analytic setting." There are, of course, few who would disagree with Sandler at this point. But I wonder how many would have disagreed with him at the time. Where did Sandler's position on this matter fit in the history of psychoanalytic ideas? I am thinking again of the manner in which Brenner was beginning to update his own view of the transference, as well as of Gill's (1982) more interpersonal view of transference and Edgar Levenson's (1972) before him, not to mention many object relational conceptualizations.

Fonagy credits Sandler with extending the concept of countertransference to "reflect the regular function of the unconscious mind," thus likening it to what we might think of as an ego function, much as Bird (1972) did with the concept of transference. It is a position I support. But was it really Sandler who made us aware of this function, or did he simply make it more legitimate in certain cultures to speak of the clinical territory Kleinian analysts had been working for many years?

To those of us more ego-psychologically minded, Sandler's conceptualizations seem so intuitively correct that we tend to lose sight of where they came from, especially since Sandler himself did not cite the contemporary Kleinians extensively and approvingly until near the end of his life. In this regard, I find Kernberg's discussion of the paper on role responsiveness particularly apt in the way he closes the circle, making clear its proximity to Kleinian conceptualizations of projective identification.

Even the concept of role responsiveness, however, has undergone some elastic change, as illustrated by several of the authors in this issue who use it in somewhat idiosyncratic ways, demonstrating again the power of the clinician's personal conceptual renderings. I am thinking, for example, of Cooper's reference to "patients who require a prolonged period of role responsiveness." It is an intriguing observation, but not what I understand Sandler to have meant by the concept. Cooper implies that role responsiveness is something the analyst might encourage or allow consciously and selectively for varying lengths of time, when indicated for particular patients. I take Sandler's concept, on the other hand, to refer to a phenomenon that is, descriptively speaking, operating unconsciously and involuntarily to varying degrees with all patients.

Similarly, I am puzzled by Holder's notion that "free-floating attention is directed toward verbal and nonverbal communications of the patient" whereas "free-floating responsiveness" is directed toward the countertransference thoughts, fantasies, and feelings which that material evokes in the analyst's mind." I would have thought both free-floating attention and free-floating responsiveness are directed toward the patient's productions and reflect different aspects of the analyst's analyzing instrument. Perhaps Holder means that, historically, free-floating attention focused on the verbal and nonverbal data of observation whereas free-floating responsiveness is *shaped* by the analyst's countertransference in addition to the patient's internal state. Regardless of these quibbles, Sandler would, I am sure, have been fascinated by these examples of the idiosyncratic ways in which individual analysts translate bits of his theory into their own terms, and he would no doubt have considered it worthy of further study.

Broad as some of Sandler's sweeping conceptualizations were, others were offered cautiously and tentatively. Nowhere is this caution more evident than in the final published version of the paper on role responsiveness, which retains what must be two drafts of the sentence quoted by Gabbard above, in which Sandler can be seen to be hedging his bets. Consider the sentence once again, with the pertinent phrases italicized:

> I want to suggest that *very often* the irrational response of the analyst, which his professional conscience leads him to see entirely as a blind spot of his own, may *sometimes* be usefully regarded as a compromise formation between his own tendencies and his reflexive acceptance of the role which the patient is forcing on him [Sandler, 1976, p. 46, italics added].

It is left to others to decide whether the phenomenon occurs "sometimes," "very often," or perhaps ubiquitously. Lending tentative support to the last of these possibilities, Kernberg, noting that the "patient seeks to evoke a corresponding emotional reaction in the analyst," suggests "it is possible that there is always such a reaction evoked in the analyst before he becomes able to interpret." I strongly support this view, although I disagree with Kernberg's suggestion that the "importance of this results from the atmosphere created by the patient, *rather than* from what the patient says" (italics added). As with Holder's attempt to separate the "direction" of free-floating attention and responsiveness, it seems to me the analyst's responses will always be shaped by *both* the patient's words *and* the atmosphere the patient creates.

While we need to leave room for the fact that different analysts work in different ways, I have suggested elsewhere that analysts, "in a state of what we might call *countertransference readiness,* can make observations only through their own conflictual organization" and that "to state Sandler's point even more broadly . . . for analysts in their ordinary working mode, *every* thought, feeling, or action is the outcome of something stirred by the patient and their own conflictual issues." Our effectiveness depends, it seems to me, on our capacity to make use of our own activated conflict, which operates as a form of "signal conflict" (Smith, 2000, pp. 106–107).

I particularly appreciate the section "Some Future Trends" in Kernberg's contribution to this issue. To those he has specified, I would add only the following. In his 1983 paper, out of which so much work has come, Sandler wrote,

> It may be relevant to our understanding of transference if we consider that introjects are constantly being externalized, in a sense being actualized, so that they can be related to as external objects rather than as internal ones. Such a tendency to externalize one's

> introjects is probably a fairly general one, and deserves closer investigation [p. 43].

Again there is modesty in this observation. I suggest that Sandler is once more positing a universal aspect of human experience, still not fully explored, one that relates to his interest in the identity of perception, and that, if closely investigated, might lead us to a more fundamental understanding of the role of externalization more generally in psychic life, thus bringing us full circle to the point with which Freud first struggled in his 1895 "Project."

The need to match what is experienced internally with what is perceived externally might be seen as an essential aspect of mind, applicable to wish fulfillment, to be sure, but also to the perception of reality in general, that is to the very nature of perception itself. Further, if we begin life governed by the principle of identity of perception, then mentalization, in Fonagy's terms, would truly represent the first developmental step into a different world.

I am extremely grateful to *Psychoanalytic Inquiry* for the invitation to contribute to this discussion, to the six contributors for their generous papers, and, posthumously, to Dr. Sandler for the stimulation of his ideas, his tolerance for argument, and his courage to question and to integrate what many had elected to avoid. His loss was enormous, but so was his impact, and the generativity of his ideas will be felt for many generations to come.

REFERENCES

Bird, B. (1972), Notes on transference: Universal phenomenon and hardest part of analysis. *J. Amer. Psychoanal. Assn.,* 20:267–301.

Brenner, C. (1982), *The Mind in Conflict.* New York: International Universities Press.

_______ (1994), The mind as conflict and compromise formation. *J. Clin. Psychoanal.,* 3:473–488.

_______ (2002), Conflict, compromise formation, and structural theory. *Psychoanal. Quart.,* 70:397–417.

Busch, F. (1992), In the neighborhood: Aspects of a good interpretation and a "developmental lag" in ego psychology. *J. Amer. Psychoanal. Assn.,* 41:151–177.

Deutsch, H. (1926), Occult processes occurring during psychoanalysis. In: *Psychoanalysis and the Occult,* ed. G. Devereux, New York: International Universities Press.

Fonagy, P., Target, M., Gergely, G. & Jurist, E. L. (2002), *Affect Regulation, Mentalization, and the Development of the Self.* New York: Other Press.

Freud, S. (1895), Project for a scientific psychology. *Standard Edition,* 1:295–397. London: Hogarth Press, 1966.
Gabbard, G. O. (1995), Countertransference: The emerging common ground. *Internat. J. Psycho-Anal.,* 76:475–485.
Gardner, M. R. (1991), On oscillation and other matters. *J. Amer. Psychoanal. Assn.,* 39:851–870.
_______ (1995), Recollections: Sexuality, neurosis, and analysis. In: *Hidden Questions: Clinical Musings.* Hillsdale, NJ: The Analytic Press, pp. 76–99.
Gill, M. M. (1982), *Analysis of Transference, Vol. 1.* New York: International Universities Press.
Gray, P. (1986), On helping analysands observe intrapsychic activity. In: *Psychoanalysis: The Science of Mental Conflict,* ed. A. D. Richards & M. S. Willick. Hillsdale, NJ: The Analytic Press, pp. 245–262.
Grinberg, L., Sor, D. & Bianchedi, E. T. (1977), *Introduction to the Work of Wilfred Bion.* New York: Aronson.
Hamilton, V. (1996), *The Analyst's Preconscious.* Hillsdale, NJ: The Analytic Press.
Joffe, W. G. & Sandler, J. (1967), On disorders of narcissism. In: *From Safety to Superego,* ed. J. Sandler. New York: Guilford Press, pp. 180–190.
_______ (1968), Adaptation, affects and the representational world. In: *From Safety to Superego,* ed. J. Sandler. New York: Guilford Press, pp. 221–234.
Levenson, E. A. (1972), *The Fallacy of Understanding.* New York: Basic Books.
Michels, R. (2003), The several relationships of theory and practice. *Psychoanal. Quart.,* 72:275–285.
Racker, H. (1968), *Transference and Countertransference.* New York: International Universities Press.
Rangell, L. (1988), The future of psychoanalysis: The scientific crossroads. *Psychoanal. Quart.,* 57:313–340.
Sandler, J. (1960), The background of safety. In: *From Safety to Superego,* ed. J. Sandler. New York: Guilford Press, 1987, pp. 1–8.
_______ (1962), The representational world. In: *From Safety to Superego,* ed. J. Sandler. New York: Guilford Press, 1987, pp. 58–72.
_______ (1976), Countertransference and role responsiveness. *Internat. Rev. Psycho-Anal.,* 3:43–47.
_______ (1983), Reflections on some relations between psychoanalytic concepts and psychoanalytic practice. *Internat. J. Psycho-Anal.,* 64:35–45.
_______ (1987), The concept of projective identification. In: *Projection, Identification, Projective Identification,* ed. J. Sandler. Madison, CT: International Universities Press, pp. 13–26.
_______ (1990), Psychoanalytic dialogue between Joseph Sandler and Evelyne Schwaber on "The Value and Function of Theory in Clinical Work: The Relation of Theory to Clinical Data-Gathering," presented to the American Psychoanalytic Association, New York, May.
_______ Dare, C. & Holder, A. (1973), *The Patient and the Analyst: The Basis of the Psychoanalytic Process.* New York: International Universities Press.
_______ & Joffe, W. G. (1969), Toward a basic psychoanalytic model. In: *From Safety to Superego,* ed. J. Sandler. New York: Guilford, 1987, pp. 235–254.

_______ & Sandler, A.-M. (1983), The "second censorship," the "three-box model" and some technical implications. *Internat. J. Psycho-Anal.,* 64:413–425.

_______ & _______ (1984), The past unconscious, the present unconscious, and interpretation of the transference. *Psychoanal. Inq.,* 4:367–399.

_______ & _______ (1987), The past unconscious, the present unconscious, and the vicissitudes of guilt. *Internat. J. Psycho-Anal.,* 68:331–341.

Schafer, R. (1968), *Aspects of Internalization.* New York: International Universities Press.

Schwaber, E. A. (1992), Countertransference: The analyst's retreat from the patient's vantage point. *Internat. J. Psycho-Anal.,* 73:349–361.

Slap, J. W. & Levine, F. J. (1978), On hybrid concepts in psychoanalysis. *Psychoanal. Quart.,* 47:499–523.

Smith, H. F. (2000), Countertransference, conflictual listening, and the analytic object relationship. *J. Amer. Psychoanal. Assn.,* 48:95–128.

_______ (2001), Hearing voices: The fate of the analyst's identifications. *J. Amer. Psychoanal. Assn.,* 49:781–812.

_______ (2003a), Common and uncommon ground. *J. Amer. Psychoanal. Assn.,* 51: 1311–1335.

_______ (2003b), Conceptions of conflict in psychoanalytic theory and practice. *Psychoanal. Quart.,* 72:49–96.

_______ (2003c), Theory and practice: An intimate partnership or a false connection? *Psychoanal. Quart.,* 72:1–12.

Spillius, E. B. (1992), Clinical experiences of projective identification. In: *Clinical Lectures on Klein and Bion.* London: Routledge, pp. 59–73.

Valenstein, A. (1973), On attachment to painful feelings and the negative therapeutic reaction. *The Psychoanalytic Study of the Child,* 28:365–392. New Haven, CT: Yale University Press.

Wallerstein, R. S. (1988), One psychoanalysis or many? *Internat. J. Psycho-Anal.,* 69:5–21.

_______ (1990), Psychoanalysis: The common ground. *Internat. J. Psycho-Anal.,* 71:3–20.

17 Hammond Street
Cambridge, MA 02138–1915
henryfsmith@cs.com

Joseph Sandler's Quiet Revolution: A Discussion

JOSEPH D. LICHTENBERG, M.D.

I center my discussion of the papers in this issue of *Psychoanalytic Inquiry* on Peter Fonagy's evocative proposal that Joseph Sandler's theories were crucial for a "quiet revolution" in psychoanalysis. The writers in this issue are unanimous in their praise and appreciation of Sandler's many contributions. I consider the validity of characterizing Sandler as a pivotal or transitional theoretician, especially as his work bears on the contemporary shift from a one- to a two-person psychology.

ALEX HOLDER COMMENTED THAT GIVEN JOSEPH SANDLER'S PROLIFIC writings "it cannot have been an easy task for the Editor of this issue of *Psychoanalytic Inquiry* to select just three papers containing some of Sandler's key concepts." Holder's comment reminds me of the conversation Mel Bornstein and I had in planning an issue to honor Sandler's remarkable contribution to psychoanalysis. Too big to cover all—what shall we focus on? Looking back, I recognize that my contribution to the final selection was based on the three concepts that most impressed me: safety, a representational world, and role responsiveness. These concepts occupy a permanent place in my thinking, albeit in an altered form to accommodate my departure from the language Sandler used to describe them. Keeping the evocative power of the terms while reframing their meaning—a sleight-of-hand

Joseph D. Lichtenberg, M.D. is Editor-in-Chief of *Psychoanalytic Inquiry.*

trick conjured to link the past to modern day—meshes with Sandler's presentation of his theoretical innovations. Each of our authors' comments on this aspect of Sandler's writing exemplifies the "quiet" approach Peter Fonagy depicted of Sandler's revolutionary thinking.

Sandler's innovations span the entire psychoanalytic field, and in a remarkable survey Fonagy provides access to and critical assessment of them. Fonagy's paper conveys the scope of Sandler's ideas: the representational world; the concept of feeling states; the superego, the ego ideal and the ideal self; pain and depression; the background of safety; a theory of trauma; the basic psychoanalytic model; actualization and role responsiveness; internal object relations; projective identifications; the three-box model; unconscious fantasy; transference; countertransference and the vicissitudes of guilt; regression; and contribution to epistemology. Taken as a whole, this massive project demonstrates Sandler's brilliance and his ambition. Our contributors highlighted their particular favorites from Sandler's comprehensive coverage of the psychoanalytic field.

Fonagy tell us that "Sandler revised psychoanalytic theory by placing feeling states rather than psychic energy at the center of the psychoanalytic theory of motivation." At a time when American psychoanalysis was dominated by Hartmann's neutralization, Sandler asserted that subjective experience in the form of feeling states represents a state of self in relation to another person. Fonagy aptly notes that Sandler thus bridged classical drive and object relations theories, "Affects drove wishes, which in turn drove actions, and could be seen at the root of conflict." For Sandler, the avoidance of anxiety was no longer at the center of motivation but rather the pursuit of safety. "Safety," Fonagy writes, "is the most radical example of Sandler's rethinking of motivation in terms of feeling states in place of drives." Thus, "the pursuit of safety is an overarching construct, compatible with instinct theory, that has the capacity to organize defenses, perceptions, and fantasies." The object plays as important a role as the self in the mental representation that embodies the wish. Object relations are thus fulfillment, not only of instinctual wishes, but also of the needs for safety, reassurance, and affirmation.

When a patient's representation of the object contains unwanted aspects of the self-representation, the patient attempts to make the behavior of the analyst conform in actuality with the distorted representation. Consequently, analysts should allow themselves a free-floating responsiveness, whereby they accept—at least in part—and reflect on the role assigned to them and put it to good use in understanding their patients.

References similar to those culled from Fonagy's comprehensive survey can be found in each of the papers in this issue. In fact, each author praises a cherished proposal of Sandler's many theories and clarifications. Otto Kernberg emphasizes the link to object relations, Glen Gabbard to countertransference, Holder to the clarification of affect and projective identification, Arnold Cooper and Bornstein to clinical experience. The clarity of Sandler's writing is apparent in the consistency of each author's writing. The limited variation that does exist lies in weighing Sandler's overall place in the psychoanalytic field.

For Fonagy, Sandler's meticulous, systematic development of the representational world framework was the bedrock of the "quiet revolution" in psychoanalytic thought. The balance of radical reconceptualizations clothed as minimalist innovations was the hallmark of Sandler's brilliant contribution. Fonagy sees Sandler as a bridging force in psychoanalysis who attempted to find the inherent linkages between opposing ideas, and helped to close the gap between American ego psychologists and British Kleinian and object relations theorists. Through representation and the desire for safety, Sandler created a profoundly different environment for developing theory and practice. He prepared the groundwork for the emergence of psychoanalytic relational theory and for considering the actual relationship between patient and analyst as primary organizer of therapeutic thinking. "Suddenly there was room for Kleinian ideas of projective identification, British Independent ideas of the holding environment, North American object relations concepts as well as self-psychological ones," Fonagy writes, and a refocus on the Sullivanian interpersonalist approach. In other words, Fonagy sees Sandler as a major transitional figure for leading us to our current age of pluralism and diversity.

Similarly, Kernberg regards Sandler as having "contributed more than anybody else to the integration of classical ego psychology with contemporary object relations theory." Sandler's stress on the interactional nature of the desired, wishful object relations, and the influence of unconscious desire on the actual behavior of the significant other signifies a shift from one-person psychology to a two-person psychology.

Gabbard puts a slightly different spin on this: "With [Sandler's] solid common sense, his impressive synthetic mind, and his carefully reasoned style of argument, he demonstrated that both a one-person and a two-person psychology are relevant to psychoanalytic theory and practice" (not a shift to a two-person psychology but a one- and two-person psychology). Gabbard cites Sandler's concern that projective identification had become an all-encompassing term that had lost its specificity. Sandler argued that the complicated system of unconscious cues involved in an analyst's response (countertransference) was not adequately explained by the term projective identification. Through his detailed description of role responsiveness and actualization, Sandler foreshadowed a current understanding of enactments and engagements as inevitable and valuable components of therapeutic action.

Holder includes Sandler in the following group of analysts who have revised the development schema: Bowlby, Stern, Emde, Kernberg, and Fonagy. Their similarity lies in their emphasis on affects. Holder, like our other authors, notes Sandler's observation of the tenacity with which patients adhere to past traumatic object relationships based on the sense of safety these patterns provide despite their debilitating nature. This theme is exemplified in the clinical vignettes of Cooper and Bornstein. Sandler, in 1990, described intrapsychic "dialogues" between the self and an object which, although painful, persecutory, or guilt-making, let the patient feel safety by allowing the continued presence of the safety-giving object in fantasy.

Cooper's and Bornstein's clinical examples present troubled patients who establish an exchange in which the analyst feels left out while the patients remain exclusively involved with a fantasy object in their representational world. In time, as the result of analytic exploration and openness to role responsiveness, the patients established a discrepant or alternative object relationship in which the analyst obtained a safety-giving place in the patients' representational world. In their actual relationship, analyst and patient experienced the analyst's presence.

The previous vignettes illustrate the essential nature of Sandler as a major contributor to psychoanalysis. He was first and foremost a clinician; thus a human existential element underlay the theoretical cleansing and proposing. The nonexperiential had to be relevant to the experiential as in the three-box model.

About 20 years ago, I invited Sandler and other senior analysts to present process notes of actual clinical exchanges to Washington Psychoanalytic Society and Institute analysts. Although well received by most, two of the institute leaders commented that the presentation sounded more like a conversation than an analysis. Sandler looked puzzled and answered, "Isn't that what analysis is—a conversation, a dialogue?" Sandler's reply was in keeping with what he had written (quoted by Holder):

> The analyst is, of course, not a machine in absolute self-control, only experiencing on the one hand, and delivering interpretations on the other, although much of the literature might seem to paint such a picture. Among many other things he talks, he greets the patient, he makes arrangements about practical matters, he may joke and, to some degree, allow his responses to depart from the classical psychoanalytic norm. My contention is that in the analyst's overt reactions to the patient as well as in his thoughts and feelings what can be called his "role responsiveness" shows itself, not only in his feelings but also in his attitudes and behavior, as a crucial element in his "useful" countertransference.

The next morning at breakfast, Sandler told me he continued to be troubled by the criticism and wondered what possible problem or danger could be attributed to ordinary human responsiveness. In a quotation selected by Bornstein from a 1984 paper written with Anne-Marie, the Sandlers wrote:

> A major analytic goal is to get the patient to become friends with the previously unacceptable parts of his self. . . . To do this means that the analyst has to provide through his interpretations and the way he gives them an atmosphere of tolerance of the infantile, the perverse, and the ridiculous . . . an atmosphere which the patient can make part of his own attitude toward himself, which he can internalize along with the understanding he has reached in his joint work with the analyst.

All of the authors in this issue relate Sandler's theoretical contribution to theoreticians who came before, his contemporaries, and modern-day. Several cite him as a quiet revolutionary who serves as a transitional bridge to the present. What does it mean to be a transitional figure? In a recent book, Teicholz (1999) portrayed Kohut and Loewald as providing a transitional bridge to postmodern theorists. Similar claims for being major transitional contributors could be (and have been) put forward for Winnicott and Bion.

Referring to Sandler or to any other important analytic contributor as transitional implies ambiguity in the evaluation. The consistently positive statements of our issue's authors about Sandler's contributions to psychoanalysis indicate that if it were not for his transition work, later steps in the field would not have occurred. On the negative side, there was a step to be taken that the theoretician came right up to but did not take—like Moses leading the Israelites to the promised land but never getting there himself. Of course, in psychoanalysis, no promised land exists, only a continuous process of changing perspectives. Both the positive meaning (Sandler's work was a necessary link for changes in perspective) and the negative (a further step possible to take was not taken) can be argued.

Safety was already in the analytic vocabulary in the work of Bowlby on attachment when the infant seeks a secure base at times of danger and loss. Sandler's concept of safety as an emotion extends the meaning to safely affecting every aspect of psychic life, thus leading to a marked change in perspective. Representation was being delineated in ego psychology and expanded by Jacobsen. Sandler's representational world gave the concept a more generally humanistic aura. Role patterning was borrowed from sociology, and Sandler gave it a highly sophisticated role in psychoanalytic theorizing. Through role responsiveness, Sandler made possible a clarification of processes involved in enactments and engagements that have occupied many theorists subsequently and provided an alternative to or an enrichment of projective identification—a very valuable bridging contribution that is, to my knowledge, uniquely Sandler's.

What leaps did Sandler not take? Cooper elaborates in this issue:

> In terms of contemporary neuroscience one could suggest that the representational world is a dynamic set of interrelated brain networks that are at every moment active among the entire range of brain and mental structures, including those responsible for current perceptions, implicit and explicit memory schemas,

> conscious affect states and affects that are out of awareness. They are part of the implicit and procedural memories that are currently activated, including state-dependent affective and memory arousals, as well as needs and fantasies, conscious and unconscious, that are aroused by the current experience.

He concludes, "I believe that his views were always in accord with modern nonlinear dynamic systems theory." I agree that Sandler's overall modifications of classical theory moved his views in accord with nonlinear dynamics systems theory, but the differences are noteworthy. For example, Cooper refers to implicit and explicit memory schemas, implicit and procedural memories. In my work I describe motivational systems, others refer to self and interactive systems of regulation, patterns of disruption and repair (Beebe and Lachmann, 2002), implicit and explicit relational learning (Stern et al., 1998). Sandler may be said to have implied and included all of these ideas, only stated in a different vocabulary. However, the main distinction lies in current systems theories' fuller appreciation of the intersubjective nature of all experience. As noted, Gabbard sees Sandler holding to both a one-person and a two-person psychology while Kernberg ascribes a shift into a two-person psychology. My view is Sandler was a two-person clinical and theoretical process theorist loyal to an intrapsychic (one-person) focus for explanatory constructs. Unconscious fantasy was the anchor that kept his theories attached to an intrapsychic formulation.

All of this issue's authors point to Sandler's revisions based on an altered revitalized theory of affects. With it he could create, change, and yet hold to a drive-conflict model by continuing to ascribe a crucial significance to unconscious fantasy and the resulting distortion. Adherence to a drive-conflict model has consequences for the nature of representations. Sandler wrote at a time when the object representation was believed to come into being as the goal of wish or desire. At this time in theory making, differentiation, separation, and individuation were viewed as the essential processes of development and self- and object representations were conceptualized as distinct entities, introjects, and internal objects.

A contemporary perspective of a representation formed as interactional had yet to come into prominence. This perspective was largely the result of intersubjective theories of Trevarthen (1977) and Stolorow and Atwood (1992), representations of interactions that have been generalized (RIGs; Stern, 1985) and internal working models (Bowlby, 1980). Sandler's role responsiveness not only is compatible with an intersubjective perspective, it requires it. Similarly, Bornstein notes that the three-box model requires a subjective perspective to account for how "we live with others, while we live within ourselves." Sandler straddled this issue by describing a child's coping approach to attachment as becoming internalized in an internal object relationship affecting later interactions with others while also referring to introjects and internal objects as more static entities.

The quiet side of the quiet revolution implies caution, and caution is not unexpected in a theoretician who emphasized the salience of safety. Sandler and each of our contributors have achieved distinguished careers, maneuvering in a world of politics—of psychoanalytic politics. This fact is acknowledged in each of the papers, although I don't believe the word "politics" is ever used. As Fonagy and Gabbard note, Britain with its three-in-one society presented the outsider, the non-British-born Sandler, with one set of pressures, and the larger world of psychoanalysis, America, Europe, and South America, presented another.

As Editor of the *International Journal,* Sandler demonstrated he knew the value of caution and appreciated creativity. In an informal discussion of our career paths, Joe said to me it is wise not to speak out too early—an excellent bit of advice that was too late for me to take. I can imagine that had he lived he might have taken his view of unconscious fantasy and explored, revised, and reset it in a subtle but revolutionary frame of lived experience, implicit and explicit memory, and relational learning and multiple presymbolic and symbolic coding of interactions. But he would have continued to tread lightly because in that way he was able to make a powerful contribution not possible for a more provocative theoretician.

Constructing theory his way built the bridges all of our authors applaud. It is no small accomplishment to have been, as Gabbard notes, "a role model within the British Society for the maintenance of intellectual rigor while also allowing for peaceful coexistence of different theories and cross-fertilization from one theory to another."

REFERENCES

Beebe, B. & Lachmann, F. M. (2002), *Infant Research and Adult Treatment: Coconstructing Interactions*. Hillsdale, NJ: The Analytic Press.

Bowlby, J. (1980), *Attachment and Loss, Vol. 3*. New York: Basic Books.

Stern, D. N. (1985), *The Interpersonal World of the Infant*. New York: Basic Books.

_______ Sander, L., Nahum, J., Harrison, A., Ruth-Lyons, K., Morgan, A., Bruschweiler-Stern, N. & Tronick, E. (1998), Non-interpretive mechanisms in psychoanalytic therapy: The "something more" than interpretation. *Internat. J. Psycho-Anal.,* 79:903–921.

Stolorow, R. & Atwood, G. E. (1992), *Contexts of Being: The Intersubjective Foundations of Psychological Life*. Hillsdale, NJ: The Analytic Press.

Teicholz, J. (1999), *Kohut, Loewald, and the Post-Moderns*. Hillsdale, NJ: The Analytic Press.

Trevarthen, C. (1977), Descriptive analyses of infant communication behavior. In: *Mother–Infant Interaction,* ed. H. Schafter. London: Academic Press, pp. 227–270.

6256 Clearwood Road
Bethesda, MD 20817
joelichtenberg@aol.com

Epilogue

By remaining focused on clinical data and the basic clinical concepts of psychoanalysis, Joseph Sandler developed a pluralistic approach to psychoanalysis at a time when psychoanalysis was burdened by a polarization of models and theory. Sandler was one of the few analysts of his time who contributed to the onset of the changing face of psychoanalysis. His gift has helped psychoanalysts define a vision of a pluralistic psychoanalysis for this century.

Melvin Bornstein, M.D.
Issue Editor

Note. An inaccurate version of "What's Going On with Dora? An Interpersonal Perspective" by Emily A. Kuriloff, Psy.D that compromised the clarity of the author's meaning was published in Volume 25, Number 1. It will be reprinted in its entirety in Volume 25, Number 3.

